GARDEN OF LOVE

18 Stories to Inspire Love, Hope and Joy

HEARTFELT AND INSPIRING STORIES
BY 18 INTERNATIONAL AUTHORS
TOLD FOR THE VERY FIRST TIME

Angela Mah , Chrissy G. Tasker , Dr. Ankit Agur

Archana Chawla , Dee Khanduja , Dr. Anita

Ho Ee Kid , Ian Maxwell, Jenny Wang, May Quan Ho

MeenuAgrawal , Monika Khanna, Nishith Bhatnagar

Karen Saunders, Sargun Bedi, Tammie Horton, Vinson Chua ,Vera Lim

Producer: Chrissy G. Tasker

The World is So Big
Publishing
www.twisbpublishing.com

Ordering Information:

Quantity sales: Special discounts are available on quantity purchases by corporations, associations, and others. For details, contact the publisher at the address above.

www.twisbpublishing.com

ISBN 978-981-14-8287-8 (E-book)

ISBN 978-981-14-9235-8 (Paperback)

ISBN 978-981-14-8288-5 (Hardcover)

A catalogue record for this book is available from the National Library of Singapore

FOREWORD

This book is written for ordinary people like you and me – tired, emotionally exhausted, overstretched, and spiritually drained from doing too many good things. Life can take any number of turns without warning. Life might be normal now, but this could change without much notice. The reality is that life can be hard and difficult. A phone call might bring bad news about illness or the loss of a job. A relationship might be broken because of betrayal and there are no good answers for the numbness and panic that grip us. If any of this sounds familiar, the book in your hand addresses similar struggles through the experiences of its writers.

Many people have helped shape the messages in this book. Their contributions bring much to the table but the common thread that ties it altogether, is love.

Everyone suffers from some physical and emotional pain in life. Medical help can bring relief to physical injury and illness. However, emotional hurt requires something different. The pain that is brought by the loss of a loved one, business failure, a broken marriage, friendship or even the uncertainty of COVID-19 is not simply medicated. Meeting the need of those who are struggling with inner pain requires a heart of love in expressing words and acts of compassion and comfort.

The sacred book defines love this way:

If I speak with the eloquence of men and of angels, but have no love, I become no more than blaring brass or crashing cymbal. If I have the gift of foretelling the future and hold in my mind not only all human knowledge but the very secrets of God, and if I also have that absolute faith which can move mountains, but have no love, I amount to nothing at all. If I dispose of all that I possess, yes, even if I give my own body to be burned, but have no love, I precisely achieve nothing. (1 Cor. 13:1-3)

The principle that can be gleaned here is that doing good must be rooted in love. We can be successful in all we do and be able to fulfil our dreams but if we do not do it with love, we have missed what really matters. There is no value in the things we are doing if they are not done in love. Generosity without love is empty. The greatest deed done without love is nothing. The only right motive for doing what we do is true love.

There might be many reasons that point to the possibility that you might not make it through your difficult time but the reality is that there is no hopeless situation and that love, faith, and hope will see you through.

Rev Dr. Christopher Chern

Senior Pastor

Grace Baptist Ministries

About Rev Dr. Christopher Chern

"Doing Good must be rooted in Love"

Pastor Chris left his profession at Hong Kong Bank in 1994 and transit into full-time ministry work. He has been pastoring the congregation at GBM since 1994. He graduated from International Baptist College (IBC) in Tempe, Arizona (USA) with a M.A. in Biblical Studies and was ordained in 1997. In 2012, He received his honorary doctorate of divinity (D.D.) from South India Baptist Bible College & Seminary.

His wife is currently a home-maker and an excellent cook! They have two daughters: Charissa, and Cheryl. He enjoys playing racket games and jogging with his wife and friends.

You can reached Pastor Christopher at office@gbm.sg

TABLE OF CONTENTS

ABOUT GARDEN OF LOVE

Have you smelled the flowers lately?

When was the last time you stopped and observed the ladybug resting on the flower bed?

The theme of **Garden of Love** is inspired by nature. We chose this theme as Nature offers limitless motivation if we're willing to pause and savour the wonders around us. Pause, let the beauty sink in and nature work its magic. Your life will bloom with contentment and fulfilment.

Garden of Love is a beautiful amalgamation of life journeys of 18 authors and their transformations. It encompasses many traditions and voices, and offers insight on pain, struggles, and love. Each voice is accompanied with passion for life and passion to inspire and bring hope to your life.

These stories moved their souls and now inspire others to transform and evolve stronger and braver! Each story speaks of Love, Joy, Hope, Faith, Wisdom, Perseverance, and Victory; urging readers to stay vital and in love with this life, no matter the hardships.

With much love and compassion, all the proceedings of sales will be forwarded to I-India – A charity that provides care, love, and development for children and communities living on the streets of Jaipur in conditions of extreme poverty. They strive to help as many children as possible and focus on those in most urgent need.

I-India was established in 1993 and currently reaches over 3000 children daily through their street schools, residential homes, and vocational centres. This non-governmental organisation (NGO) in Jaipur assists children with immediate challenges, such as homelessness, child labor, malnutrition, and illness, while also developing their attitudes and skills in a way so that they have greater choice to transform their future. To find out more about I-India, visit: https://i-indiajaipur.org/

ABOUT I-INDIA

I-India's mission is to provide care, love and development for children and communities living on the streets of Jaipur and in conditions of extreme poverty. We strive to help as many children as possible and focus on those in most urgent need.

It was established in in 1993 and currently reach over 3000 children daily through our street schools, residential homes and vocational centres. The non-governmental organisation (NGO) in Jaipur assist children with immediate challenges, such as homelessness, child laborers, malnutrition and illness, while also developing their attitudes and skills in a way so that they have greater choice to transform their future.

Philosophy:

- Help as many children as possible
- Focus on those in greatest need
- Do not discriminate or avoid difficult cases

Strategy:

- Create a comprehensive system of services to fulfil children's long-term needs for education, skills, and emotional support, as well as their short-term needs for nutrition, health and shelter.

- Maximise the impact of this system through integrating programs, monitoring and improving the quality of service, and seizing opportunities to expand.

A LOVE POEM

By Sargun Bedi

I was rushing

To break-free amidst this sailing spree

Was that my courage or my hope?

The day I understood this, I eloped

Not literally but inside my mind

I was shattered and wanted to be kind

I found pit-holes and what not

I kept asking myself 'what is it that I have got?

While challenging was the only option

I knew I couldn't let myself rot

Did I drop my guard? I did

Was I stuck like the dart? I was

I kept wishing that If 'I were'

I wouldn't be where I was

This journey of moment by moment screech

Was silently shunting me in its breach

What came by was the experience

To let me in society's adherence

Did I feel myself or was I numb?

I kept searching. How dumb?

Those, who taught me this, were a bunch of rule setters

My race was not with them. I craved to be a go getter

My dialogue with myself amazed me

I was wise enough, it saved me

For all that I kept hunting outside

That very bit taught me

To start looking for love inside

I am oddly young, bold and even old

But love taught me to always be a child

I endure my path of cracks

For it taught me to unpack

Unpack all that, that didn't make sense

I gathered love within me, my garden and fence

I gathered love within me, my garden and fence

I welcome to handhold whoever enters in

I make self-love a priority over surrendering

If you are looking for external acceptance

Come here, I'll be your reflectance

I am Garden of Love

I am Garden of Love

A symbol of peace, flying around like a happy dove

With Love

Sargun Bedi

About Sargun Bedi

Sargun Bedi is an Author, Counselling Psychologist, Behavioral Trainer, Powerleap Coach, Facilitative Speaker, Creative Writer and Founder Director of **Lucid Mind** - a service brand that offers a platform of soul searching and self-development in an empathetically valued zone.

She has 9+ years of practice and professional experience in mental health and training sector. She facilitates and empowers people facing everyday challenges of life. With the help of her advanced counselling skills and therapeutic interventions, she aims to help people reach their balancing mechanisms and unravel their potential that is hidden behind the window of pain, confusion and regret.

Her forte lies in the minute observations and scientific methodology to understand humans in various settings, carving out ways in bringing the needed paradigm shift in the society at large. Her eclecticism is dynamically solution focused, keeping the humanistic base stronger and analytical base sharper.

Besides this, she has authored a book named **Life-A Mixed State** that portrays various life domains through poetry and co-authored a book named **Revive & Thrive** that reflects her own teenage journey of acquiring wisdom through emotional struggles. She also has research papers published in UGC journals. She has come a long way whilst gaining international existence towards her content.

Her formula towards happiness is to treat ***'actions' as habits.***

You can connect with her at lucidmindservices@gmail.com

Website: www.lucidmind.in

LinkedIn: https://www.linkedin.com/in/sargun-bedi/

Instagram: @lucidmindcounselling; @coachsargun

HERO AND VILLAIN

By Dr. Ankit Agur

Remember when you were young, your parents would be there, looking out for you, constantly taking care of you, and love you, no matter what? When you achieved something, they would teach you to be humble and grounded. When you were upset, they picked you up and encouraged you. They kept a check on you till you were balanced from within. Even when you made mistakes, they punished you untill you learn your lesson. And the lessons that you've learned from them more often than not make you who you are today. The lessons—good or bad—define what purpose you choose to pursue in your life. So does life teach you the most important lessons in balance?

Many times in the course of our life, we want to embrace pleasure without pain, optimism without fear, happiness without sadness, laughter without tears. We run away from the painful events and memories. Run away from our past if it hurts us, and feel anxious about our future, thinking the past will repeat itself. Our fears drive the major decisions in our life. Fear of failure, fear of rejection, fear of not being good enough, fear of not looking good enough, fear of expectations, fear of loss, fear of unpleasant gain, and many more fears that drive most of our unconscious life decisions. Oddly though, while running away from fears, we look to be the complete opposite, and try to be positive, think positive, suppress our pain, and always be optimistic. We read self-help books, take courses, pick mentors who pump us up and keep us in high energy, and try to surround ourselves with people we admire and respect to apparently imbibe their qualities. The entire personal development industry thrives on our insecurities. Eventually, positivity becomes a driving force in our life and yet our journey of running away from negativity continues.

In due course, you realize that these fears, pain, and anxieties suppressed within become fermented over a period of time and keep showing up when you least expect them, in a way that's most traumatic, and you express them toward the people closest to you in particular. The more positive you want to become, the more issues crop up in your life when you least want it. And people feel depressed, thinking that they've done everything they can to turn their life around, and still, life pushes you down and messes you up. That's when people fall prey to mood disorders like bipolar, depression, and various other mental illnesses that are symptoms of false perceptions rather than a definitive medical diagnosis.

Yet you still are like a ping-pong ball, seeking help from one area of study to another. And get disillusioned with life and begin resenting it.

And where do the life lessons I told you about come into picture? Look at the most important moments in your life, the ones that define your strengths, your character, and your resilience. These so-called challenges and moments of desperation are those that you wish you never had to face. The biggest legends and the most inspirational figures throughout history have reached that point due to the most pressing and pressurizing situations that forced them to awaken from their slumber of ignorance and embrace the situations in front of them to work through their fears and limitations relentlessly till their mission matched their vision.

After going through stressful initial years in medical school, I have been a product of positive thinking, gratitude, and self-motivation to the point of resenting myself whenever a negative thought came in my mind. Every time I failed, I blamed myself for not being motivated enough rather than digging deep to find the roots of these occurrences. I was resisting my intuition to face my fears and drawbacks, and somehow believed that if I didn't think about my past it would go away. Resentment turned to shame, and shame turned to low self-worth, and low self-worth to hatred toward myself. And long before I realized, I broke down to the point of not accepting my very self. At that lowest point, I decided to be true to myself and accept myself as a whole with all the imperfections in my body, mind, and heart. I learned the beautiful ways in which embracing my most despised parts helped shape the wonderful guy I am today and how they made me stronger yet introspective, bolder yet sensitive. More important than anything, my children and wife adore me for who I am. It felt really empowering to appreciate the villain and the hero in me and their significance in my life. Liberating to the point of me now feeling unstoppable in every area of my life, be it being medical director for a hospital, an author, a transformational speaker, resilient coach and a loving hands-on, proud dad. When I owned my villain and my hero, I discovered *myself*.

I have realised that being positive has a by-product of dissociating ourselves or running away from things that hurt us and make us feel anxious, guilty, shameful, undeserved, unrewarded, resented. Being positive is like renovating the interiors of our minds without paying attention to addressing the very foundation. True empowerment is when we accept and embrace the role of pain in our lives and understand the benefits it gives us, appreciate it as much as pleasure, and feel grateful for having helped us become what we are. That is when we truly become balanced and live a life of fulfillment and equanimity. You no longer have to face your demons because you'll realize that your demons are actually angels in disguise. When you love the good as much as the bad in yourself and others, you live through the most magical moments in space and time. Our true potential is revealed to us.

"A diamond is formed as a result of extreme pressure over a prolonged period of time. If you want only a mild and gentle pressure, you'd be at best an intricate work of clay in the hands of a skilled potter."

It's only when you truly embrace and be grateful for every moment that you are living through do you truly realize the beauty of even the most challenging times. Steve

Jobs got kicked out of his company before he came back and established Apple as a force to reckon with in the tech world. Sam Cawthorn had to go through the most devastating of accidents where he lost his dominant upper limb and permanent stiffness of his right knee, before he *bounced forward* and established himself as an authority in inspiring thousands of people to be their most authentic self through the art of speaking. I'm sure each one of us would love to have their accomplishments, yet fear going through what they've been.

The first step to reach the dizzying heights in times of adversity is to most importantly take ownership of yourself. Face each and every perceived fear in your life. I'm not asking you to be brave and positive while facing your inner demons. I simply ask you to have faith in the universal Love that is there to guide you to express your innermost potential. And just like a mother shows tough love to teach the most valuable lessons, so too does the Universe show you such challenging circumstances to help you find your path to access this potential and live a life true to your nature thriving in all your genuine glory.

The second step is to understand and be grateful for everything in your life. Gratitude is the most powerful and yet the simplest way to be in harmony and sync with the world around you. Gratitude brings you back to your heart and helps you appreciate and seek opportunities usually hidden in plain sight. To be grateful is to be in Love with the varied hues of causality and eventuality in nature.

The third most important step is to see the good in the bad and the bad in the good. Both good and bad can't exist without one another. There's no heat without appreciating cold, no day without night, no pleasure without appreciating pain, no beauty without appreciating the ordinary. The world is a play of contrasts, and it would be foolish to wish for one without the other. Same goes for people. When we are polarized toward either an apparent good, or in other words infatuation in others, we lose ourselves to them and put them on a pedestal, to the point of living in their values in life. When we are polarized toward apparent bad or negative things in someone, we are again polarized and put them down, force them to live in our values, and expect them to do what we think is important. When we see the good in the bad and the bad in the good, we see them at a level that we're on, and that's when our true authenticity shines through. When we have a heart-to-heart conversation with everyone in our family or at work, the relationships, personal or professional, blossom. And when we are in our authentic self, no problem is too big, no challenge too daunting, and relentless resilience is born.

The most beautiful nature of our existence lies in the awareness that the Universe is always in a state of flux. It's so amazingly dynamic that the purpose and direction of the flow evaded the most fertile minds of our generations and the past. It is because of the shoulders of these giants and a blessed few that we are now in a better shape to comprehend that the Universe is a play of equilibrium. The subjective good and bad when seen from a universal scale is a catalyst to make our thoughts, actions, and intentions in line with our most inspiring purpose in life. Our destiny ultimately is defined by these loving nudges from the Universe in our life and our environment. When these loving nudges turn to shove, pandemics arise. And we are, in a way, lucky to witness the complete expression of the tough love from our Universe.

COVID-19 is a great equalizer. It has made the world a level playing field for everyone who is willing to own, acknowledge, and embrace their true nature and work toward and from their most innate potential. Being a doctor and having colleagues who've worked the forefront, trying to help the population, it's a constant feedback that the severity of symptoms and outcome of the disease in patients is highly unpredictable. Those who are young and have no associated illnesses have been found to fall prey to it, and those who are older with comorbidities have been found to be doing well. The trends have been quite baffling. No science can explain the paradox till now. After careful observation, and after numerous discussions with my colleagues, we inferred that those who were balanced and equanimous from within and those who are living a life congruent to their highest values are most likely to have milder symptoms and recover faster than those who are otherwise. It can be attributable to the fact that they have lower levels of the stress hormone cortisol, which in turn increases immunity. Definitive research still needs to confirm our observations. It's fascinating to see such a synchronous amalgamation of all the different fields of study, which proves that ultimately the more balanced you are, the more optimal your state of being.

The faster we are aware of the implicit nature of the apparent chaos and challenges in life, the more cantered we are, and the decisions and action we take in our life will be more in alignment with our highest purpose. I personally love the way the same was said by our ancestors in Vedas, theorized by philosophers in ancient Greece, and now proven through quantum field theory. You know you are one step closer to knowing the absolute truth when you intuitively feel certain of everything you've experienced and put together in life. Moments of serendipity where our intuitions, spirituality, science, and research come together to paint a dazzling picture of the marvellous ways of the divine.

Universal divine Love is always guiding us to be our most authentic self. Not because you can't be any better, but cause you're the best being who you truly are! A balance of the best hero and the most magnificent villain.

About Dr Ankit Agur

Dr. Ankit Agur is a Thought leader, An Author and World's leading authority on PROFECTION. He is also an Orthopaedic Surgeon specialising in Arthroscopic surgeries, Managing Director of AGUR PRIME HOSPITALS and a motivational speaker.

He hails from a small town in one of the most backwards districts in South India. Coming from a conservative background from family of doctors, he has had to overcome many traditional ideas and break free from shackles of expectations to truly understand, realise and embrace his life purpose.

Over the course of the last 10 years being an Orthopaedic and trauma surgeon, he has witnessed extremes of human physical pain. Yet, it is the pain of the human emotions and the flaws of our patterned social conditioning is what drove him to break away from his mould and dive deep into the intrinsic wisdom and extrinsic knowledge to truly let his authenticity shine by spreading the power of PROFECTION and impact the lives of people around him.

He shares a magical connection with his two unplanned yet extremely loving children. And it is this special bond which he shares with his daughter and subsequently his son, that inspires him to be the best version of himself and truly BE and SPREAD abundance in the world.

Instagram:- dr.profectionist (https://www.insta-gram.com/dr.profectionist/)

Facebook:- https://www.facebook.com/Dr.Profectionist

AWAKEN THE WARRIOR WITHIN

By Vera Lim

Great Leaders who left a legacy for future generations.

Heroes and Heroines who saved the world.

I have read stories of great leaders making a stand for a cause they deeply believed in and willingly sacrificed their lives for it.

In the movies of superheroes, stories were weaved around individuals who were once a nobody, yet they found inner strength and willpower to overcome all odds and fight for their world.

Inspired and motivated…

I aspired to be like them one day…

Yet, deep down, I felt that I was a nobody…

I will never be that hero or heroine…

Worthless, Unloved and,

Ordinary…

There was nothing special about me that was worth mentioning about…

I was like any other Ordinary children,

With an Ordinary childhood….

My Ordinary Life

My father was born during a period of economic depression after World War II. My mother was born during an increase in births following the end of World War II, called the "Baby Boomers" generation.

As the second daughter in the family, I was born in 1979, a Generation X baby. As reminisced by my mum, I was such a "big" baby that there was speculation that she might be having twins in her womb.

On the day I was meant to arrive in this world, I gave my mum a hard time. The doctor took a while to "pull" me out. When I finally came out and was carried over to her, she saw a big red patch on my left leg, running down from my buttocks to my ankle. She was worried sick as she thought I was hurt during the delivery. Since then, she was continually fussing over my left leg to ensure that it would grow well.

Ever since I was born, I lived in a 3-room flat in a high-rise building with my parents and squeezing in a room with my elder sister and then later, my youngest sister till adulthood. During my childhood, I remembered my parents sharing stories of them living in attap houses in a kampong. They came from a big family with about ten siblings, and life was simpler than.

I did not have much chance to interact with my grandparents, as they passed away long before I was able to meet them or understand as a child. The only little memory I had was my father's mother, who stayed with us for a few months every year on a rotational basis between his brothers. She had severe diabetes and was not able to walk and move on her own, so we took turns taking care of her.

Even though my parents struggled with survival during their growing-up days, they made sure that our basic needs were well taken care of. While we may not be financially wealthy, my parents had never once let us feel that we lacked in our basic needs. We had a roof over our heads, food on the table to eat, and nice clothes to wear.

Our simple joy came from the occasional birthday celebration at MacDonald's or KFC. Those were the days when dining at fast-food restaurants was a big thing for us!

Overall, growing up in our small 3-room flat and having neighbours around our age to play together with, my childhood was considered a happy and enjoyable one.

An Empty Feeling Within

Yet in this Ordinariness of life, a deep, empty feeling began to form within me...

When did it happen?

I had not much idea.

Vague memories of some childhood incidents came to my mind.

"Your ears are so wide open, like elephant ears!"

Friends, relatives, and strangers would tease me, and some would even pull my ears.

"What is this red patch on your leg? Why was it so red?"

Someone will be commenting and passing remarks whenever I wear shorts, skirts, or swimming costumes.

It seems like everywhere I go, there will be something to say about my physical outlook. Maybe this was the only way adults knew how to strike conversations with children. Being a quiet and shy little girl, I tried hard not to be bothered by it.

A Suppressed Teenager

As I got older, I became more and more conscious of my physical body.

"Your eyes have no double eyelids."

"You have a flat chest."

I started to feel awkward and ashamed of my body.

I wanted to hide it…

I hid my big red birthmark below pants…and I would hardly wear skirts, shorts, or swimming costumes in public…

I hid my ears behind my hair…and I would rarely tie up my hair…

I hid my flat chest behind loose blouses…and I would not wear body clinging clothes…

I became easily sensitive and upset over the words of others.

Yet, I did not know how to express my feelings.

I felt a deep sense of sadness. I felt belittled by others. Tears would well up in my eyes, like pressured water in a dam, waiting to be released at any moment. Being brought up in a family where I was not taught how to communicate my emotions and thoughts, I silently held back my tears and fight back my feelings.

A few more years went by, the sadness was still there, a deep gnawing feeling that was slowly and silently eating away at my happiness.

Being a teenager did not make my life any easier.

In studies, in beauty, in whatever I do, I was being compared with others, and it seems like I was never enough.

Craving for love, acceptance, and friendship, I went around trying to fit in.

I wanted to be part of a popular group in my school so that I could be seen.

I wanted to be a humorous person so that people would like to be with me.

I wanted to be what others want me to be,

Yet I was slowly…

Slowly losing myself…

Amidst the sadness, there was anger secretly brewing within me. I wanted to vent my frustration and unhappiness.

I secretly wanted to go against whatever my parents told me to do.

I quietly rebelled against the people around me by wanting to be different.

Instead of being a good and well-behaved girl, I failed my exams on purpose…

I played truant in school together with my friends…

I made my relief teacher cry by writing sarcastic jokes about her on a note…

I changed…

"Who am I?"

I did not know who I was anymore…

I did not know what I was doing   anymore…

For years, I had been putting on a mask, pretending to be somebody that I am not…

Forcing myself to be outspoken when I am quiet and shy…

Forcing myself to be a clown to cheer people up when I did not like to be in the limelight…

Forcing myself to smile when I was still feeling sad and empty inside…

I said, "Yes," when I actually wanted to say "No"…

Everything I did, I went against my heart…

Everything I did, I went against my conscience…

"Who can understand me?"

My heart was calling out…

My heart was calling out for someone to listen to me…

My heart was calling out for someone to understand me…

I looked in the mirror…

I could not bear to see my face in it…

I could not lift my eyes to see and face myself in the mirror…

The sorrow that was clearly written on it...

The guilt...

The hate...

I hated myself...

I hated who I am...

I yearned for someone to be able to see me for who I am...

I yearned for someone who could love me for who I am...

I yearned for someone who could accept me for who I am...

Who can I trust?

Who can I confide in?

There was nothing much in my family and my country that I could look forward to...

There was nothing much from the people around me that I could rely on...

I wished I could get out of my cage...

To see the world out there and not be tied down by my home and my country...

I yearned for the freedom to do what I want...

To make my own choices and be free from the clutches of what the society wanted me to be...

My Chance, My Opportunity

Year 2001 marks a significant turning point in my life…

An opportunity came while I was searching on the internet.

I found something meaningful yet adventurous for me.

It was a youth development expedition to Namibia, organised by Raleigh International.

Namibia, a country in Southern Africa…

A remote part of the world which I had not much knowledge of…

What I had briefly understood from a documentary was the living conditions of the people on the other side of the globe, with not much food to eat, water to drink, and proper place to sleep in.

This was my chance to free myself and to see the world!

At the age of 23, I made my first major life decision to resign from a full-time job to volunteer in Namibia, South Africa, without seeking consent from anyone, including my parents.

This was the beginning of my life journey…

Finding Myself

In October 2002, my quest to explore began.

Throughout my three months of an expedition in Namibia and one month of backpacking in Cape Town, South Africa, my mind was opened by what I saw.

Plain porridge for daily meals, sweets were a luxury for the children, women subjected to the risk of contracting HIV, and poverty drove people to resort to violence to survive.

During my backpacking trip, I encountered a robbery while preparing to travel to a new place with a friend. Both of us were threatened at knifepoint by a group of teenagers, and we were robbed of our money. The teenagers looked fearful of their actions and quickly scrambled away after getting what they wanted. Then, my heart went out to them. All that I had experienced and seen with my own eyes greatly disturbed my mind.

One question kept bothering me deep within my heart,

"Why am I here in this world?"

Having felt small and insignificant throughout my life, I desperately wanted to find the answers to my question. With this question in my heart, I aimlessly wandered into a run-down bookstore in Cape Town, South Africa. As my eyes scanned through rows and rows of books on the shelves, a tattered book caught my eye. My hand reached out to it and turned to the cover of the book; it was titled, "My

Land and My People." My gut instinct told me that this was the right book for me as I flipped through the pages to look at the description. Holding this book tightly in my hands, I could not wait to reach the backpacking lodge I stayed in.

Back at the lodge, I found a safe, quiet space on the balcony. Making myself comfortable on a rattan chair, I began to read the book, page by page, sentence by sentence, word by word. A sudden immense, deep emotion swelled up within me as I was reading.

Tears started to stream uncontrollably down my face.

The deep compassion and love that the person in this book had for his thousands and thousands of people who depended on him had touched my heart in a way that no words could describe. He was truly a great leader whom the people in his country had relied on with strong faith and devotion.

In my heart, I said a quiet prayer of aspiration to become like him someday.

My Teacher, My Guide

February 2003, this was the year that I was back in my home country after the expedition. This was also the year that SARS hit my country and the people around the world.

Finding difficulty in landing myself a job, I struggled mentally to keep my spirits up. Fighting my constant restlessness and worry, I suddenly felt even more deeply that I did not know what I wanted in life. My initial excitement of being able to make decisions for my own life and having the freedom to do what I wanted became dim in comparison to the darkness that was weighing heavily in my heart.

I felt insecure…

Uncertain…

Lost…

Who am I?

Why am I here for?

It was during this time of uncertainty that a kind-hearted friend reached out to me. She invited me to attend a teaching by a spiritual teacher. Internally, I resisted and was skeptical about it. I was stubbornly telling her that I would not stay if it were not suitable for me.

On the fateful day of my first meeting with this spiritual teacher, I walked up to him after his teaching. As I looked up at him, he smiled at me gently, reaching out his hand to touch my face, he said,

"I understand you."

The tears that were stored up for so long suddenly burst open.

His compassionate gaze seems to reach the deepest, darkest part of my soul that no one could see.

His compassionate speech seems to know the words that my heart yearned to hear.

His compassionate touch seems to know that I needed love.

At this moment in time, I felt like I have found a teacher for life.

A teacher who could understand me and love me for who I am.

A teacher who could guide me to find answers to the questions in life.

I am forever grateful to my friend, who was the bridge that connected me to my spiritual teacher.

As for the book which has inspired and touched me deeply, I found out later that it was an autobiography of His Holiness, the 14th Dalai Lama, the Spiritual Leader of the Tibetan People, and the Tibetan Buddhist Tradition, which was the direct lineage of my spiritual teacher. Thus, I slowly realized the profound significance of this connection between the great leader in this book and my spiritual teacher.

No words can fully describe how deeply blessed and fortunate it has been for me.

A miracle has manifested in my life...

For the first time...

And the journey to find the answers to my life questions began...

A Life Lesson Learned

"Why do I feel that I am not worth people's love?"

This was the first question that I asked my teacher.

And his answer was,

"No one will know how to love you unless you know how to love yourself."

How to love myself?

What can I do to love myself?

His answer left a deep imprint in my heart, and to date, it remains a guiding principle on how to live my life.

Evolve, To a New Me

Like a caterpillar needs to go through an evolution to transform into a butterfly; a journey of self-transformation requires a willingness to go through it. Throughout my life, I have been searching for love, externally. No matter how much love others may have shown me, it was never enough. The evolution process was both healing and insightful as I discover who I truly am.

Connect Within and Without…

As I learned to be in touch with myself, connecting, and relating to others became easier as I could be more empathetic, understanding, and kind toward others. I slowly came to understand that when we cannot love ourselves, no one will know how to love us the way we want to receive it.

What was Learned from this Life Lesson?

1. Be Gentle with Ourselves

"When we can be gentle with ourselves, we can be gentle with others."

Self-hate has made me my worst enemy. Harsh self-judgment and criticism are continually playing in my mind. It made me worry and overthink a lot until I felt so crippled and paralysed by it. Self-doubt and self-sabotage became a shadow that followed me everywhere. Whenever I started any project or tried to manifest an idea into reality, I would pull the handbrakes and question myself if I could really make it happen and be successful.

What can we do about it?

Try using a notebook as a journal to pen down any negative thoughts and feelings when they arise. By finding a way to express our emotions that is both safe and healthy, we practice being aware and mindful to avoid behaviours that will cause harm to oneself and others. Writing is also a good way to declutter our minds to create space for more objective reflection after we are done with writing down our emotions.

2. Have Compassion for Ourselves

"Show compassion to ourselves when we face our demons within."

Setting high standards for ourselves will lead to an increase in our fear of failure. When writing down our emotions in a journal, we need to be aware and mindful to free ourselves from judgments.

What can we do about it?

Facing ourselves takes courage, and being compassionate to ourselves is most needed at this point. Give ourselves loving, kindness, time, and patience to go through this healing process. We may be feeling full of anger, hurt, shame, jealousy, or guilt. It is okay. It is okay for us to feel whatever it is that arises. Acknowledge our feelings and remind ourselves that there is no right or wrong about it.

3. Forgive Ourselves for all our Past Mistakes

"To move forward in life, we need to forgive ourselves."

Many of us, including myself, have an intellectual understanding that we need to let go of the past so that we can create a better future for ourselves. Yet, forgiving others, and more importantly, forgiving ourselves seems to be the most daunting task to do. Our pride and ego cannot bear the thought of knowing that we have made a mistake. We choose to sweep it under the carpet than to look at ourselves honestly.

What can we do about it?

Learn to view our mistakes objectively and subjectively. Holding onto our mistakes is more painful than facing up to it. By recognising an undesirable habit or behaviour as separate from ourselves as a person, we can avoid judging ourselves as a "bad" person. Practice analysing our situation to understand why and how we made that mistake so that we can make better decisions for ourselves in the future.

4. Accept Ourselves for our Imperfections

"Everything is impermanent; nothing is perfect; we are all a Work in Progress."

Idealism, Perfectionism, Setting high standards for ourselves.

This is how I once was, and I expected people around me to keep up with it. Expectations will eventually lead to disappointments whenever others fall short of it. This is also the cause of undue pain and hurt for ourselves and others.

What can we do about it?

By learning to love and accept our strengths and our weaknesses, we stop focusing on the "wrongs" and instead are able to view all situations and challenges as an opportunity to help us to grow. Learning to rejoice in our growth will help us to gain more self-confidence and be a better person every day!

5. Never Give Up on Ourselves

"No matter what happens, Never, ever give up on ourselves."

Even when it seems like no one can understand the pain that we are going through,

Even though it seems that we are in the deep, dark, rock bottom of the ocean,

By just having one person who can understand us and believe in us,

By our own faith and trust not to give up on ourselves,

we will be able to find the inner strength within us to go up again.

This human body is precious. Our lives are precious even when we may not see it, especially when our pain and sorrow blind us. Be willing to make a conscious decision to take charge and be responsible for our lives.

There is a Warrior within us waiting to be Awakened.

"In the darkest moments,

when we can face ourselves courageously,

to make friends with every fear,

to overcome any obstacles,

to fight any internal battle,

to make a conscious choice,

to live a meaningful and purposeful life,

With time,

With patience,

With resilience,

With discipline,

With every step,

We will slowly and surely, **Awaken the Warrior Within Us.**"

About Vera Lim

Vera Lim is a Relationship Coach, Trainer and Author who strives to advocate deep, meaningful conversations within ourselves and with others to build strong children and families.

Parenting with Vera is born from a deep commitment to give voice and action to this cause.

To bring families together to spread more love, peace, and harmony in our world.

In the last 20 years, Vera's love for working with people has led her to interact with thousands of people: from business owners to aspiring entrepreneurs, from married couples to single parents, from children and to youths. All of them were from diverse walks of life with different life challenges.

In all her interactions with the people, there was one thing in common:

Everyone wants to Feel Heard and Be Understood

She has found out that to truly build strong relationships with others, we need to first have the Courage To Go Within ourselves.

Today, more than ever, with the rising mental health issues around us and the social media affecting the way we live, she felt an even stronger urgency to bring about an Evolution to deepen human connections at home, in our work and the world.

Now is the time that we come together as a community to grow the courage to go within ourselves. Join her in Parenting with Vera as we walk a reflective and mindful journey to Grow At Our Own Time and Space!

Facebook: https://www.facebook.com/groups/parentingwithvera

LinkedIn: https://www.linkedin.com/in/veralim-109b0873/

Website: https://www.bebigbyvera.com/

BEYOND THAT WELL

By Jenny Wang

A bed of roses

Have you ever wished that your life was a bed of roses? Do you ever wish that you can indeed be happy, and your life can be smooth sailing? As we look around us, especially on social media nowadays, we often envy others who seem to have an incredible life – blissful family, outstanding achievements in their careers, and whatnot. I am sure someone else is green with envy about YOUR life too. But wait a minute, do you ever feel that your life is as wonderful as perceived by others? I did not. In fact, life can be a bed of roses, but roses come with thorns. Life is full of obstacles; it is about how we overcome them. In this chapter, I will share how I have coped with 'thorns' on the roses, finding hope, and rediscovering myself.

***

"Is she the one who topped the secondary two cohort this year?" Someone whispered to her friends as she took a quick glance at me. I have never received so much attention from peers in schools, and it became an added burden on me.

'Achiever' is one of my top Gallup[1] strengths. Since I was young, my ability to excel in academics is akin to a secret weapon that a superhero has to win all challenges. In a typical household in Singapore, most parents would want their children to do well academically. In the 1980s, most of the parents came from a humble background, and they would think that studying hard to achieve good results would set a good foundation for working in adult life. Have you ever felt that this notion has deceived you? The world has changed so much over the last three decades! No one knows that having a certificate would not necessarily get you a good life. Neither did we know that the United Kingdom is out of Eurozone, and Donald Trump is the president of the United States. Similarly, one cannot see the possibility of the future and should not be afraid to take a step out of your comfort zone. Who knows, you might be surprised at how much you can learn and that deep sense of fulfillment that cannot be measured by monetary gains.

---

[1] https://www.gallup.com/cliftonstrengths/en/252137/home.aspx

My life journey thus far has appeared to be smooth sailing, and one will be surprised that I received a diagnosis of depression. Just two weeks ago (at the time of writing this chapter), my cousin and friends were appalled when I shared a post on Facebook that I had a difficult transition from high school to junior college. Why was it difficult for me? From one who was deemed to be very capable, I became a student who could not answer simple questions during lessons.

"What is centripetal force?" Mr. Ang, who was a tall, bespectacled young man who just graduated from the National Institute of Education, asked me with enthusiasm. "I don't know about that. I only know the phrase: May the force be with you!" I answered with a chuckle because it felt great to make the whole class laugh and see the dismal look on my poor physics tutor.

Junior college was a horrible time for me. I was an excellent student during primary and secondary school, a grand total of ten years. When I entered one of the top colleges in Singapore, I became a small fish in a big pond, or should I say an ocean. I wasn't close to my classmates; most of them were from well-known high schools while I was from a neighbourhood school. I scrapped through my first year of college, and in the middle of year two, I was asked to drop a subject. Perhaps it was for "my own good" since I was told that I couldn't cope. I didn't feel that I was given any recognition and encouragement from school or home. Like a scene from the movie "Inside Out[2]," my island of achievements and happiness collapsed. Yet, the fighter in me nudged me on. I told myself that I must prove to others that I am capable of doing well in academics. The 'mugger' in me was ignited. My life was tripartite of study-sleep-eat until the end of my A-levels examinations.

A Frog in the Well

My life has been focused narrowly for the first three decades. I wished I had spent time developing other aspects of my interests. When I was young, I could draw well and play piano with one hand after listening to the melody. Yet, I didn't further develop any of these interests. I only managed to learn how to cycle in my twenties after I bought a bicycle. In my early thirties, I have yet to know how to swim, crippled by both my fear of failure and intense focus on work.

One of the characteristics of achievers is that we work hard and possess a great deal of stamina. We take immense satisfaction in being busy and productive. I saw an interesting word in an urban dictionary some time ago – *'stress-laxing,'* verb: being stressed, so that relaxing makes you more stressed because you are not working on what

---

[2] Inside Out is a 2015 American 3D computer-animated comedy film produced by Pixar Animation Studios and released by Walt Disney Pictures.

makes you stressed. I shared this on Instagram and gar-nered several responses again. It looks like I am not the only one who experienced this. It is a typical issue that most people face nowadays. One of my friends com-mented, "Isn't this a panic attack?" I replied, "Panic at-tack is worse." But I didn't add – I had that before.

My career as a teacher has been incredible, and to many, I had excellent prospects. My students loved me, and my boss and colleagues had been great, too. Within four years, I earned a promotion to the position of Subject Head. If many people deemed me a workaholic when I was a regular teacher, I was worse when I got promoted. It wasn't because I wanted to have more monetary gains. In fact, I often forgot that my salary was deposited into my bank account. I was one of the first few to get into school in the morning and the last few to leave at the end of the day. Weekends were not relaxing either. I spent most of my time working in a café, and I even managed to get its gold membership. You can imagine how much coffee I drank! I am a *coffeeholic* too. At times, I also helped a small group of students on weekends to catch up with their work. In the midst of my hectic schedule, I didn't pause and ask myself what I truly wanted. There was a deep sense of fulfillment when I managed to finish my work and see my students graduate with flying colours.

It was 11 pm on one of the nights of the year 2010, and I was still working on my laptop. My parents came in and asked me to sleep. "I can't. I can't seem to think properly, and I can't finish what I need to!" I said with a hint of panic and began to sob shortly after. This scenario repeated several times until one day in early 2011; I really couldn't pick myself up to go to work in the morning. I felt defeated and upset. The more I couldn't accomplish what I intended to, the worse I felt.

I stared at the ceiling as I lay on my bed. I felt tears rolling down my cheeks. Several thoughts came to me:

"What is the meaning of life?"

"Who am I working so hard for?"

"My brain couldn't function today. How am I supposed to deliver good lessons?"

I sat up on my bed with a heavy heart and cried uncontrollably. I was single ever since I stepped into the teaching profession. I felt lonely, and I didn't manage to share my worries with my peers, as most of them think that I am overreacting.

Ultimately, I had to see a doctor at a nearby clinic. Frankly, I wasn't sure it was the right diagnosis; the doctor said that I was suffering from depression, and he prescribed medication and one week of medical leave. Little did I know that this was going to be a long-term medication! I returned to work with a decision that I am going to quit teaching. It was a sudden yet decisive move. However, I did stay until the end of 2011, as I felt that I needed to be responsible for my graduating students. That year, I stepped down as a Subject Head and focused on teaching. I felt better, but there were still lapses of downtimes. I also managed to find another job in another field. I thought I would recover for sure.

***

A step forward and half a step back

The year 2012 seemed to be full of hope for me, although I had a pay cut. New job, new colleagues, new challenges. I thought my life would change for the better just because I changed my environment. According to the job description of my new job, it involved learning design using Infocomm technology. I thought my past experience as a competent and award-winning teacher would land me in good stead. Instead, life continued to throw curve balls at me. The person who interviewed me didn't turn out to be my boss. My new boss told me that I did not have a Master's degree, and hence, I couldn't do such learning design work. I ended up doing more of a supportive role for training programmes that I named an "IT Support Officer." After two weeks, I felt like quitting again.

"Aren't you glad that you do not need to work over the weekends now?" My friends asked me.

"No, in fact, I felt 'useless' working in such a 'low competency' job," I said.

While I did not have a relapse of depression, I was unhappy. Ironically, I missed teaching and often think how the new ideas that I have during this job stint would be carried out in the classrooms. Every day, I was just going through the motions in life. There was no passion, and soon enough, I thought I should go back to teaching again. At this point, some of my friends were puzzled and questioned my decision.

I was lucky that I landed myself a new teaching job in a new school quickly, just after half a year of exploration in another industry. This time around, I am just an 'ordinary teacher. Life should be a breeze, right? The achiever stake in me sabotaged myself again, and I stuck out like a sore thumb (for good performance) for doing more than what I should. I awarded opportunities to teach talented classes. Within four years, I had the chance to lead a team. My pride grew bigger such that I must do everything with excellence. I cringed at other people's work when it fell short of my expectations. I was in angst or upset when my lesson didn't go well. My definition of failure threshold level became so low that I must have a fun and engaging lesson every single time! I was taking things personally. I didn't realise that a student who dozed off during my class wasn't because my lesson was boring, but instead he did not have a good sleep the night before. I didn't know that I was performing at 120% of what an average person would. My life, once again, revolved around work, such that I compromised not just my health, but also my social circle. I hid in my study room after school and rarely communicated with my family. While I sulked at home, I faked a bright smile during lessons, to ensure that it was engaging for my students. Every day I was on stage, doing performances and hoping for encores. I thought my happiness was dependent on my work performance. I craved recognition and acknowledgment from bosses, colleagues, and students.

I was still taking my medication then. However, I did not have a serious relapse for years, and I thought it would be a good time to cut out the medication, which my doctor agreed. In fact, it was during this period that I met my husband and was about to get married in 6 months. That one step that I took back in 2011 was in the right direction, but I took half a step back by going back to my old behaviour. It was easy for me to stay inside the *well*. It was comfortable, indeed, until a storm came and nearly drowned me.

***

Tipping point

Every year in March, national examinations results will be released. Typically, it would be a happy day for me because a conscientious and competent teacher would deliver excellent results, right? To my disappointment, the results of my 2017/18 cohort of students released in March 2019 were below my expectations due to a myriad of reasons that I couldn't explain. I felt that I had failed my students, and I slumped back into depression. I thought it was unfair because other teachers' students did better, although they didn't work as hard as me. It was a mix of angst, disappointment, and bitterness. There were days that I sat in my car when I reached the school in the morning and messaged my then-boyfriend (now husband) that I couldn't function again. I would actually just stare at my documents, and nothing was being processed in my mind. He suggested that I should see a counselor, rather than being dependent on medication. I was reluctant, but I did it anyway because I was desperate for help. On the surface, no one could tell I was struggling. I was still performing on the stage, with my mask on.

It was a long journey of counseling, and I was back on medication. The cycle repeats itself. Something is seriously wrong. There was one thing that my counselor said that makes absolute sense – if I didn't change my mindset and lifestyle, nothing would change. She asked me to explore new interests and do things that I have passion for. My first question was, "I have no idea what my passion is, except teaching." Obviously, it was because I didn't even explore beyond teaching. I also don't make an effort to learn new things or expand my social circle. At the time, meeting new people was daunting. I felt insignificant in front of people in other industries, and small talks were meaningless to me. I always wanted to do things that come with tangible outcomes.

The year 2019 was a tipping point for me. Because of my disappointment and relapse of depression, I decided to take a break from my leadership role (again). But this time, it was with a counselor's guidance. I took a leap of faith by heeding her advice and joined a self-development programme overseas for four days during the school term. It was a life-changing moment as I moved out of my comfort zone and met like-minded people. I had several "break down" moments during the programme, but it was meant to be, some burden was lifted off me, and I began to realise I am the only one who can change my own life.

***

Growth is a continuum

"There is no fixed level of achievement or success that will allow you to live the rest of your life on cruise control, comfortably and happily. Progress equals happiness."
Tony Robbins

I began my journey of self-development and self-discovery through other programmes, and I finally picked up swimming. To my surprise, I was able to swim after four sessions of trial and error, gulping mouthfuls of pool water in front of advanced children learners. I was no longer mindful of how I think other people may perceive me. It was just my judgment that sabotaged me. The process of learning was liberating, and this time, I can swim out of that *well*. I am no longer a frog in the well. While I spent more time in other areas of interest, it did not dilute my contributions as a teacher. In fact, I began to understand more about the importance of the well-being of students, and I was able to teach more effectively with more heart and soul. I live in the present moment, and don't wait until March every year to determine my self-worth. I had more self-love as I discovered more wonderful traits about myself, and it is not a sin to have weaknesses.

I used to say, "Everything happens for a reason." But I did not fully internalise its meaning. Would I go back to the past and change anything? I won't. If these events did not happen, I wouldn't be my current self. I would not be able to share my story and bring hope to people who could be having a similar experience.

I am no longer ashamed of my condition. I am on the route to full recovery. I want everyone with such conditions to know that they are not alone, especially those in the education industry. I understand your struggles, and it is okay to feel overwhelmed.

While we light the pathway for our students or anyone you love, we shouldn't consume ourselves like a candle. Think of yourself as a rechargeable battery for that light source. To be sustainable, we need to recharge ourselves.

These are three learning points that I would like to share with you that could bring you greater clarity in rediscovering your new path when the path you are on seems obstructed.

1. External validations do not determine your self-worth. You are your own cheerleader and barometer.
2. If you find yourself trapped in a vicious cycle of unhappiness, do something different, and explore other aspects of life. If it feels uncomfortable, you are probably on the right track because change is never comfortable.
3. It is never too late to change; it matters that you start to make that change.

Things happened for a reason. Then, you would have felt the pain, and it felt that it was never going to go away. Such emotional pain is like an innate alarm system that prevents further damage. It is screaming: you jolly well better change the way you are thinking and behaving!

Should I continue to think the way I did and refuse to step out of my comfort zone, the cycle will just repeat itself. Indeed, if I continued to work in the first college at that inhumanly level, I would never move on and have the opportunity to meet my husband. If I continue with my old definition of success, I would never find new joy and interests, meet new people, and find that life is full of opportunities. You can start with your journey of "progress" and hence, achieve happiness. You are not alone!

About Jenny Wang

Jenny is a passionate educator with 15 years of experience, winning the hearts and minds of both colleagues and students of diversified learning needs with her energy and inspirational ideas.

She firmly believes in the holistic development of the next generation to empower them with relevant skills to face the ever more challenging future. She adopts active student centric learning techniques to make learning fun and engaging for her students.

In recognition of her dedication and highly qualified skills, Jenny was awarded multiple national awards such as NIE

Caring Teacher Award 2010 and a finalist for the Outstanding Economics Teachers Award 2018.

Instead of focusing on climbing the corporate ladder, her quest for progress and happiness sees her immersing herself in self-development to equip herself for the changing needs to groom the next generation. She can be followed at **LinkedIn (@Jenny Wang)**.

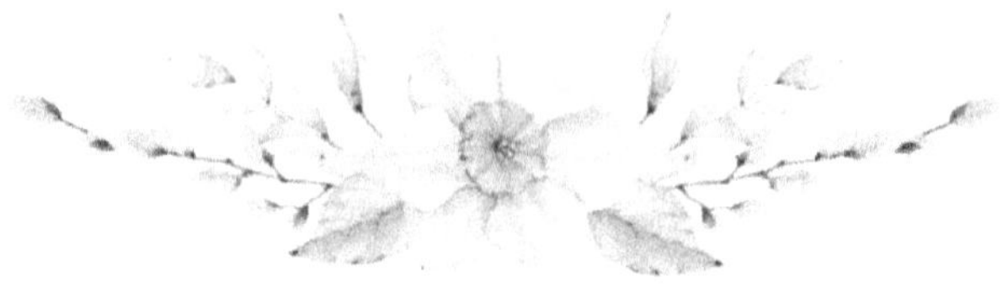

DENIAL

By Archana

She used to sit on the corner bench of my neighbourhood park every day. She comes there around 9 am, sit there for an hour or so, and then go away.

I am a retired botanist, so every day, I spend my time in the park, looking at the trees, sometimes helping out the gardener, and doing what kept me happy all my life, being with nature.

Slowly I became curious about her daily sojourns to the park; I was curious why a pretty young lady, dressed in beautiful clothes, would come and sit like that, all by herself. She would smile to herself or sometimes shed silent tears, but always immersed in her own world, indifferent to her surroundings.

It was hard to guess whether she had noticed me or not, but with each passing day, I grew more and more curious, and my urge to talk to her became greater.

Finally, I decided to go and talk to her.

I reached the park before 9 am and sat on the bench waiting for her.

Unsure of whether to talk to her or not, I saw her coming and take her usual seat on the bench as she immersed herself in her own world.

I got up and walked toward her, half dreading that she will get up and walk away for the intrusion on her privacy. I approached her and said, "Hi, I am Sager. I see you here every day."

She looked up and smiled," Me too."

"I am curious, a young lady of your age, not going to shopping malls, talking, or surfing on the phone, not even listening to music, just sitting here all by herself!"

She smiled again and said, "It's a long story."

I replied, "I have all the time in the world."

She smiled, and with an uncertain look, said to me, "I will tell you why, but you will not ask my name or my identity, and after, I may not have any conversation with you."

I was blank for the moment but was not willing to let this one opportunity to talk to her go by.

I looked at her with all my conviction and said, "I cross my heart and promise, no questions asked."

She started with a slow rhythmic voice; a distant look is in her eyes.

"I am the mother of a lovely daughter and wife of a doting husband, a freelancer. I come here and sit to figure out some things. I don't find answers, but it gives me the satisfaction of looking back and reliving the moments of my past."

Suddenly she stopped and asked, "Have you ever wondered how many people we come across in our lifetime?"

I was giving a thought to this question as she continued without waiting for me to answer.

"People come in our lives and become our friends and some mere acquaintances. There are some loves of our lives, and some enemies, too. But then there is someone who enters our life and stays there, never changing any feeling about them. They are always there, constantly, imbibed in our souls. Each thought of them is lifelong longing, a thirst which never gets quenched, and you don't want it quenched; it just becomes part of you. They engulf you in their arms, and you stay there in a state of suspension, some threshold, move a million miles without taking a single step, talk endlessly without uttering a single word.

He became that one person in my life.

When he came into my life, I never thought I was capable of love: that beautiful age, the first leg of youth, where everything seems colourful and fragrant. Going to college was a big liberation from boring school life, especially after difficult boards (school-leaving exams) – the life of freedom.

Studying hard and making a mark for myself was my only goal, and I was doing it quite successfully. I made some great friends, moments in the cafeteria, roaming around, jokes and crushes; it was sailing so smoothly. I didn't even realize when my first year was over, and in the second year came that one person.

I was walking to my department from the parking area, and suddenly a guy appeared in front of my eyes for a split second; I think someone pushed him, and quickly he moved away.

The same day after college, waiting for the bus, the same boy approached me, very confident, and asked me to be his friend. He was from the Statistics Department. I dismissed him as someone who makes some advances to woo me, routine in the college environment. But his eyes stayed with me.

He managed to cross me several times during the college hours. I started ignoring him, and he would sometimes come to the bus stand trying to talk, and after some time, I started looking for him.

I told him not to follow me but wanted to talk to him. And I guess this was the first step of denial, which would define me my entire life.

After some time, there came Valentine's Day. By then, I was already talking to him on and off, very few casual conversations, and some familiar smiles. He proposed to me with a bunch of roses, he was moving around with those, and I asked who they were for; he answered: "for me." I always saw it coming, but my heart skipped a beat at that moment; I was speechless and could not answer.

We did not meet after that for some days. I called him up early one morning, which happened to be Shivratri and we met at the college on that day. I confessed my love for him, and after that, we were officially girlfriend and boyfriend.

It was such a good time, no worries, no tensions. Those days were like surfing on a sea with winds of togetherness.

Those long talks on the phone, falling asleep with the receiver still in your hands, without disconnecting, meeting each other with the same enthusiasm and missing the person as soon as he left – this was longing.

Those long bike rides to distant places, meeting near the department in the evening, and endless stories were priceless.

We celebrated all festivals together, going to Gurudwara, celebrating Uttarayan, Holi, and Navratri.

There was new colour in Holi. The Diwali became brighter.

Navratri and Garba became more musical, dancing together, matching every step with the rhythm only a heart can recognise.

The two years just flew by.

There were fights and small separations, but that made the whole equation so alive.

Life was changing for the better; I scored good marks in the final year of graduation and joined an excellent post-grad programme.

I made my parents extremely proud of me. Somewhere some false pride seeped into me as he struggled academically, there were small differences in attitude, but love was there, still fresh and engulfing.

Then there was a sudden jolt, the world around me came crashing down; everything was shattered.

My world of innocence, love, and belief was snatched away from me. I lost my life that day, I lost my Father. Something inside me changed; my emotions were not there; each step was a burden of walking a thousand miles. Storms were ravaging my world, and everything was standing still from outside.

Did it take a toll on our relationship? Yes, without saying anything to each other, everything changed. I was not myself anymore; I could not recognise the person I became.

He was there standing steady as a rock, lending a shoulder for me to cry on. A friend to solve all my problems.

He understood my pain and tears, which I never shed, hidden under a steely demeanour of a brave girl.

Broken from within, a picture of strength from outside; somehow, he understood my complexity, which I never understood. His being there for everything made me take him for granted.

I made this hard shell around myself, too absorbed with me, so angry with the world around me, silent in a strange manner.

He was there by my side, but I was not there, could not acknowledge his being there, an escapist who wanted to run away and live in the world which was in my head, not in reality.

I lost my ability to love; he slipped by, and finally, it was over from my side as if the love he gave was an illusion.

I cheated him while running away from myself. I ran away from him, forgetting that I was incomplete without him.

Life moved on; love happened again, blessings came, and I was blessed with the best husband and friend with whom I fell in love with, again and again. But part of me was still missing; it was with him, tucked closely to his heart.

Always there with my every breath, with my every moment. He is there in my existence.

Sometimes I wonder would life be different IF?

She got up with a jerk as if some alarm woke her from her dreamy sleep.

Grabbed her purse and looked at me,

She muttered something barely audible,

Thanks for listening,

And with steady quick steps, she turned away never to return.

I sat there pondering, what IF?

Felt a pain of losing my silent friend, I was sure she walked out never to return...

Through time, love has had a lot of enemies. Religion, caste, social strata, familial enmity; these I can count at the tips of my fingers, I am sure there are more.

Yet there is one more potent than all of these, one that is much underrated, and, if truth be told, the most dreaded in times today.

That enemy is Unsaid; nothing has torn people apart more than this much-feared fiend.

About Archana Chawla

"I don't possess any special talents. I am passionately curious......"

Archana is a Medical Microbiologist and Passionate science communications professional. Currently working as, a Science Communicator for a Science Centre, she believes that science is difficult till the time it is well explained. She started her career in a Medical College as a Lecturer, later on joined one of the most reputed Diagnostic Facility of India and excelled in Microbiology Living by the ideology that nothing can substitute quality. She also worked on WHO project and was instrumental in the start-up of a Microbiology Laboratory.

Besides she is a trained Kathak dancer and a poet. She enjoys writing short stories and painting in her free time. Her passion for dressing right... makes her design her own clothes. Fashion and style is all about comfort and being relevant, and she believes beauty is in character and being unique "Only thing in life that you regret are the risks you didn't Take..."

1. Facebook - https://www.facebook.com/archana.chawla.98

2. Twitter – https://twitter.com/archanachawla12/status/1277445591765676032?s=21

3 LinkedIn - http://linkedin.com/in/archana-chawla-23b5a921

HOPE IS IN THE HEARTS OF HEROES

By Tammie Horton

In 2013 I hit rock bottom; I was utterly broken; some would argue I still am. I had become someone I didn't recognise and who I didn't want to be anymore. Since then, I have figuratively set myself on fire and have risen from the ashes of my former life. Now, I am living the life I was born to live ... but this hasn't always been the case.

I have experienced anxiety and depression since I was a teenager. I have used self-harm as a coping mechanism. I have been in an abusive relationship, and I have been suicidal more than once.

I want people to know that no matter how dark the world seems, what seems like the end is just a beginning. It is possible to turn it all around when you look for embers of Hope, listen to your heart, and become your own hero.

The World Health Organisation reports that globally every 40 seconds, one person dies by suicide. Another 20 will attempt it, and 100s more will think about it. By the time you have finished reading this chapter, approximately 22 lives will have been lost around the world, and countless others will have been impacted.

Included in these numbers are people who experience mental health issues, homelessness, abuse, and countless other problems. Maybe you have felt like this, or you know someone who is feeling that way now.

We must **ALWAYS** be able to see the light. Help is out there, and there are embers of Hope that can light the way. You only have to call out 'Hey someone, come by here, I need a hand,' You might have to say it a few times before someone will listen, but eventually, someone will.

Sometimes though, we're too broken and blinded by our misery that we think it's our destiny to live with a hurtful present and a dismal past. We can lose Hope and believe we're nothing, and we suffer in silence.

I've decided … it's time … for this … to stop.

Because when we're **IN** that dark place, we have a chance to do something we couldn't have done before:

At this point of choice, we **CAN** choose a lighter path; we **CAN** look for embers of Hope, we **CAN** build a PIRE and burn away our old selves and rise up. We **CAN** be regenerated.

We might call it 'resilience' or even 'freedom.' It's the story of the Phoenix; it is my story and my vision for how you can achieve your potential.

Do you know what the legend of the Phoenix is? The Phoenix is a mystical bird that is associated with the sun and said to have magical powers. When it is approaching the end of its life, it builds itself a nest of combustible material, a funeral pyre, and sets itself alight. It is not the end of the Phoenix; it is just a beginning. It regenerates itself and spreads its wings, rising from the ashes more beautiful than before.

The Phoenix has been used throughout the ages as imagery for rebirth, regeneration, and transformation. I identify with it because, over my lifetime, there have been periods where I have had to regenerate and transform myself. Now, I use it as a way to help others who want to make changes in their life to have a different way of looking at how to create that new life for themselves.

Even if you are in the darkest place of your life, things can get better. Just how much better depends on you. Finding your Inner PHYNIX is not an easy process. It requires you to be brutally honest with yourself, and it can take a lot of work. At times, it hurts, both physically and emotionally, because you are, after all, setting yourself on fire (figuratively speaking, of course). My PHYNIX process has four stages.

Stage 1 – The Point of Choice – The PIRE – this is where you develop your self-awareness and get a better understanding of yourself. You assess all the Pain, Indignity, Regret, and Emotions that are keeping you stuck and no longer serving you. This is the starting point for transformation.

Stage 2 – Take action – the PHUEL – this is about changing the mindset, injecting positivity, re-writing the script for the movie that is playing, the film of your life. Here we take back our Power, become our own Hero, Unearth our strengths, skills, and talents, Energise our lives with motivation and well-being, and develop Language that is positive and uplifting.

Stage 3 – Create the Experience – the PHIRE – This is where we define our Purpose, making it true to the Heart, we set Intentions keeping the end in mind, take Risks and face our fears and Enjoy the process, and love what we are creating.

Stage 4 – The Regeneration – the PHYNIX – This is where we rise from the ashes to live a life that is:

P – Passionate – Living as if you are on fire from within

H – Hope-Full – Because once you choose Hope, anything is possible

Y – Young at Heart – Be open to new experiences and develop a beginner's mind

N – Noetic – We are all part of an interconnected whole – be inspired to take action to help humanity

I – Indomitable – Strong, brave, and determined

X – Xtraordinary – Why fit in when you were born to stand out.

What I want to share with you in this chapter is three aspects of the PHYNIX process taken from the PHUEL, PHIRE, AND PHYNIX stages.

Let's start with Hope. How would you define it? The definition that I love is one by Desmond Tutu, "Hope is being able to see that there is light despite all of the darkness."

When I talk about being Hope-Full, it is not some notion of blind optimism. I know not everything works out the way we want. In fact, if it did, there would never be any surprises in life, good or bad. There wouldn't be any room to grow, to learn, or to change.

Being Hope-Full increases your problem-solving skills because you are willing to look at different options and are more inclined to give ones that are outside of the box a go.

Clinical drug trials are an excellent example of the power of Hope. Some recent studies of antidepressants began to doubt their performance when compared to a placebo in double-blind, randomised clinical trials. In clinical trials, where the placebo was engineered to produce side-effects like the actual medication, the performance of the placebo was similar to that of the medication given. People weren't taking the drug at all, but they were still getting better.

Even in the darkest of times during his internment in concentration camps during World War II, Victor Frankl observed the power of Hope in those who were imprisoned with him. Between Christmas 1944 and New Year's 1945, the camp's sick ward experienced a death rate beyond all previous experience. This was not due to a food shortage or worse living conditions, but because the majority of prisoners had lived in the naïve Hope that they would be home again by Christmas. When this Hope was not met, prisoners found no reason to continue holding on; they had nothing to look forward to. When a mind lets go, so does its body.

According to Frankl's observation regarding the higher death rate, Hope is a choice. Hope, it appears, is capable of sustaining life. While every external factor may root against you, one single act of internal defiance can counteract it all. Hope is powerful, indeed. But however powerful, the end result is never guaranteed.

In 2008, I had what I termed a nervous breakdown. I was in a relationship that was emotionally, psychologically, and financially abusive, but I was able to get by because of my three girls and my work. My workplace was my respite, a place to get away. All that changed when I had a manager that started to treat me the same way as my husband was. It was the straw that broke the camel's back.

Little did I know, while I was trying to battle with my darkness, my eldest daughter had already been fighting her own. She had experienced a traumatic event a few years before that I didn't know about and had started to self-harm. When I had my breakdown, she felt she had to be a brighter beacon to guide me back because my daughter needed my light to help her through; so, she stopped self-harming for a while.

When she felt that I was strong enough, she allowed her light to dim, and she slipped into the dark world of depression and returned to self-harming. I remember she said to me once after watching the movie, *My Sister's Keeper*, "Why won't you let me die?" It felt like my heart was breaking into a million pieces. I said to her, "Because I love you too much, and I won't let you give up Hope."

For both of us to hold onto Hope at that time meant that we had to be courageous in the face of difficulty. Both of us could have easily given up, but we allowed each other in to help. I think this is the essence of Hope – allowing others to show you the way, to be the light when all you can see is darkness. While others may not experience the same thing that we have experienced, they can show us what else is possible.

My daughter has now completed a degree in Music Performance and Composition at the Australian National University. She has been in a committed relationship for a good number of years. She has started on her journey to be a composer and to teach others to sing, passing on her love of music. She shares the story about her struggles in the songs she writes in an attempt to help others with their struggles.

When I finally left the abusive relationship in 2013, I looked for embers of Hope and found them in unexpected places. One was a lady I'd never met who ran a security company. Through one of my staff, this lady offered that if at any time I felt unsafe, I could call her and she would send people around to help.

Another was at a trivia night, hosted by a drag queen, a trivia night like no other. Over 18 months, that drag queen drew me out of my shell and got me to do things that I never thought I'd do in public.

Then, my girls bought me my first ukulele. I joined a ukulele group and had a few lessons to learn how to play. This is where my love for playing music again became ignited. I am now the Vice President of my Ukulele Club and part of the core group that performs regularly. My heart feels full every time I play.

Which leads me to your heart and what it has to say to you.

When it comes to knowing what is right for you, you have all the answers, your heart has all the answers – but you have to quiet your mind to hear what your heart has to say.

Have you heard of the saying "be true to your heart"?

The heart speaks to you with kindness and Hope. It never speaks of fear and doubt, and it will never betray you like your mind can. Your heart honours you, and when you listen to the guidance of your heart, peace and happiness is restored. Your heart holds the key to your life. Your dreams, wishes, and desires are all embedded in your heart. Whom your heart chooses to love, your life's work, and your purpose all reside here. The guiding voice or feelings of the heart have been referred to in writings and teachings throughout millennia. Unlocking this inner guidance can enable us to navigate through these changing times with more personal balance, coherence, and heart-based connection with each other.

The heart is more than the pump that keeps blood moving around our bodies. It is the first organ to form when we are an embryo, and when it stops beating, you are 'clinically' dead. Your heart is created before the brain; it is what keeps the mind alive, but it does more than that; it communicates with it in four different ways. Research shows the heart communicates through the transmission of nerve impulses; by hormones and neurotransmitters that were often only thought to exist in the brain. It communicates through pressure waves and electromagnetic field inter-actions that can be measured up to 3 feet away. Com-munication along all these paths significantly affects the brain's activity.

Research shows that messages the heart sends to the brain can also affect performance and how we see and interact with the world. I wonder if this is why some people behave differently after they have experienced a heart attack?

Your heart's energy can be felt from a distance. What you radiate out into the world can be felt by other people's hearts. Whether you come from a loving space or a fearful space, your heart's energy is constantly emitting a vibra-tion. So, when it comes to fulfilling your purpose, if your mind and heart are one, your purpose is true.

Shortly before I left public service back in 2018, I started to spiral downward again into a depression. The work that I had been doing as a certified Business Continuity Practi-tioner was outsourced to an inexperienced contractor. I was moved away from my team and overlooked for an acting position, despite having acted in the role before for two years. I felt like I was returning to the days of being bullied, and I no longer had the motivation to get out of bed in the morning. I felt like I was trapped in a whirlpool that was sucking me downward.

I had been playing around with the idea of starting my own continuity consultancy business, but I kept feeling the need to help people who were struggling with mental well-being in the workplace; this had happened many times over my career. I then realised that what I wanted to do was to ensure people's continuity. Without resilient and mentally healthy people, a business can't function at maximum potential, especially if a crisis hits.

I had a set of wings painted by an artist in Germany to represent the Phynix rising, and I was due to pick them up from the post-office on 17 September 2018. Over the weekend before this, I took time out to stop and listen to my heart. What was it that I honestly wanted to do? Did I want to stay working in an area that didn't value my expertise and dedication? Did I want to look for a position elsewhere in the government? Or did I want to follow my heart, asking for a redundancy? The heart and the mind were in agreement. Then the universe stepped in.

I picked up the wings on the morning of the 17th. When I got to work, the Branch Manager summoned me into their office. The manager and my supervisor informed me that there would be changes to how the branch operated and that they didn't know what I wanted to do. They didn't want me anymore was how I interpreted this. So, I asked for redundancy, and they agreed to it on the spot. I believe it was the universe saying, my purpose was true.

Is your purpose true? I want you to imagine you can hear the sound of a drum beating. The beat is the rhythm of a heartbeat…dum dum…dum dum…dum dum…

I want you to think about a situation that you are having trouble making a decision about or about a person with who you are having difficulties.

Now, get comfortable wherever you are, place your hands on the middle of your chest over your heart. Sit quietly and breathe. As you breathe in, imagine a light force, your inner fire radiating from your heart throughout your body. As you breathe out, radiate the feeling your inner fire gives you out of your body. Doing this will raise your vibration and help to bring your heart, mind, and body into a coherent alignment and stillness.

Be patient – it will take some time – don't let your mind give up because it will want to. Let any thoughts that come up pass away with the beat of the drum.

When you feel the stillness, ask yourself these questions:

- Does this (person, situation, or choice) represent who and what I stand for?
- Does this sound like me?
- Does this look like me?
- Does this feel like me?
- Does this excite me or make me feel more alive?

Listen to what your heart has to say. Keep going for about 5 minutes. Then, very slowly, bring yourself back into your room, lower your arms, and give them a shake. Did you get an answer? Are your heart and mind on the same page?

Reinforce your decision or feeling by grounding it with a power pose. Strike a superhero pose - feet shoulder-width apart, hands on your hips, chin tilted up, chest pushed forward.

Did you know that just holding an intentional, open-bodied pose for two minutes boosts testosterone, reduces stress hormones, increases risk tolerance, and increases the "feeling" of being more powerful — are you feeling more powerful? Do you feel like a hero? Who are some of your Heroes?

Maybe it's Brené Brown, or Mother Teresa, or Nelson Mandela. It might be your favourite sports star, a celebrity, or just someone that is close to you that has inspired you. Those might be worthwhile heroes, but it would be even better to become your own hero. Because your life is a story, and every story needs a hero. Every hero is different because every story is different. The hero of my story will not be the same as yours.

There are a few ground rules to this process of defining your hero.

Your hero has to start where you are. If you are beginning this process today, then today is where your hero's journey begins. With all the knowledge, skills, and resources you have available to you.

You have to set a time limit on when you'll become your hero. You don't have 100 years to work to get the job done ... unless you've discovered the fountain of youth ... in which case, tell us where it is … I promise we won't tell anyone.

You need a deadline for a major transformation. A reasonable timeframe is 5 to 10 years from now. At that point, you can re-evaluate and create a new hero from your brand-new starting point. But you may need to set shorter deadlines to keep you motivated so that you can see the change.

Avoid the tendency to limit yourself. You can accomplish a whole lot in 5-10 years. You're a hero, after all. So, what does your hero look like?

I want you to get a piece of paper and draw two lines, dividing the paper into four boxes. The first box is accomplishments. From this moment in time, until your deadline, what will your hero achieve? Once you're satisfied with your list, ask yourself how you could make it even better. Remember to work within the timeframe you've given yourself.

The next box is the attributes. What qualities does your hero have? What characteristics would they have to possess to accomplish everything they've accomplished? What qualities in a person do you most admire and respect?

The third box is "a day in the life." How does your hero live their life? How do they spend their day? Who is in their life? What types of activities do they do? Where do they live? What time do they get out of bed? What is important to them? Be as specific as possible.

The final box is your hero's goals. Your hero has accomplished a lot, but you are not finished. Consider what are their goals now: what do they hope for? Who do they want to become? What is their heart telling them?

Turn this piece of paper over. This is where you make your plan to become your own hero. Starting where you are right now, what do you need to do to become the hero you've defined? What changes do you need to make in your life? What goals do you need to set and accomplish to become your hero?

Consider your hero's finances, health, and fitness, social circle, accomplishments, and skills. Imagine what needs to happen to transform from your current self into your hero.

This is probably the most challenging part for most people – get started. It's fun to sit down and plan your future. It's a little harder to get busy and make it happen. You have years to complete your mission, but you don't have time to spare. The more time you wait to get started, the longer it's going to take to become your hero. There's still time to become the most incredible person you've ever known. When someone asks you, "Who is your hero?" you can honestly say, "Me, in 10 years." Be the hero of your story.

Part of my hero's story is to make the world think about the song Kumbayah differently.

I went to a Young Leaders competition, and one of the participants talked about social justice issues. She threw out the line, "I don't propose we hold hands and sing kumbayah," and that got me thinking. Why Not Kumbayah? Like the nerd I am, I did some research, and this is what I found.

It started as a spiritual plea for help from people in despair and trouble, imploring God to "Come by here" and help those who were being desperately oppressed by racial segregation in the southern United States.

It was first recorded in the 1920s and sung in a dialect called Gullah, which made "Come by Here" sound like "Kum ba yah." In 1957, a group called the Folksmiths toured summer camps, teaching the song to thousands, cementing its association with children and campfires.

In the 60's it was used as a call to action by the civil rights movement. Now, it's snarky shorthand for ridiculing the quest for common ground. But what is so wrong with seeking common ground, when even in today's society, we have people who are in despair, in trouble, and wanting to end it all.

Now is the time for us to reconnect and support one another because our very well-being depends on it. What better way is there to connect than singing songs, sharing stories, and joining our hearts?

Not only are each one of you a hero, but you are also an ember of Hope for someone. I encourage you to **BE** vulnerable, **SHARE** your stories, **REACH** out to those that need help. And if **YOU** need a hand, Come By Here and I'll help you to find your Inner Phynix, and together we can change the world.

I have reworked the lyrics as a call for us to raise our voices; to share our uniqueness and likeness. To shine as embers of Hope and to "Come by Here" when called by those who need our help.

Now I want you to imagine me playing my ukulele and singing, and you can join in.

Somebody needs you, world, Come By Here.
Somebody's calling world, Come By Here.
Somebody needs you, world, Come By Here.
Oh, Oh, Come by Here.

Join in brotherhood, kumbayah.
Join in Sisterhood, kumbayah.
Join together world kumbayah.
Oh, Oh, kumbayah.

Can you hear us world, Come by Here.
Can you see us world, Come by Here.
Can you feel us world, Come by Here.
Hear Us World, Come by Here.

I want you to remember that Hope is in the Heart of Heroes and the heroes are here, reading this book.

Ignite your PHIRE and let the PHYNIX soar.

About Tammie Horton

Tammie Horton – the Original Phynix, CEO and Founder of Phynix Initiative. She is a speaker, coach, and mental health advocate. She has a lived experience of bullying, self-harming, domestic abuse, mental illness, caring for a partner with multiple health conditions – all while holding down a full-time job and raising three children.

In 2013 she hit rock bottom, she was completely broken and had become someone she didn't recognise and didn't want to be anymore. She figuratively set herself on fire and started her rebirth, rising up from the ashes of her former life and rebuilding herself into the person she is today.

In 2018 Tammie left her career as a National Award winning Business Continuity Manager in the Australian Public Service to pursue her passion of helping people overcome distress and overwhelm through motivation and resilience coaching, educating people on the valuable skills of Mental Health First Aid and promoting social and emotional development through the use of music and rhythm.

Tammie's message of Setting Yourself on PHIRE to find your Inner PHYNIX, to live a life that is: Passionate, Hope-Full, Young At Heart, Noetic, Indomitable and Xtraordinary, is transforming lives.

My social media handles are:

Email: tammie@tammiehorton.com

Facebook: https://www.facebook.com/tammiehortonofficial

LinkedIn: https://www.linkedin.com/in/tammie-horton/

Instagram: https://www.instagram.com/tammiehorton_phynix/

Twitter: https://twitter.com/tammie_horton

SOLO CAREGIVING

By May Quan Ho

Have you ever had a moment in life where hope is the only light you see in this world?

About five years back, mum's health took a sharp decline when she experienced difficulties in digestive system ; Her frustrations began one day when she visited my family doctor. The doctor confirmed that her diet was adequate for her age of eighty. However, the cause of her indigestion issue unknown despite multiple visits to specialists at both government and private hospitals. It was finally brought under control after a year and half of doctor visits and hopping between Western and alternative medicine. She was going to the emergency room to have her pain relieved due to the chronic digestive problem , and it went from once a month to every one or two weeks! It was partially relieved after meeting her TCM (Traditional Chinese

Medicine) doctor at a private hospital. The TCM preparation has been tedious but has help her to temporary relieve the discomfort from the illness.

The next significant dip was when she started to experience the first fall on her way back home from the TCM. It was just after getting out of the taxi, as she walked over the grass patch right in front of our apartment's main entrance. It was August 2018. Eight months later, she fell on her way back to her bed around 4 am. She broke her right hip joint. The events leading up to her hip joint surgery shocked everyone in the family. She suffered delirium after her surgery and mistook my hubby's fist as a cauliflower. Next, her accelerated dementia brought her down from a healthy and sturdy figure to a frail and shaky old lady!

After recovering from her hip surgery at the nursing home, she returned home in Oct. 2019, and we hired a domestic helper. The hospital is for acute care, while the rehabilitation home is for chronic or long-term care. When she suffered her second fall in Dec. 2019, she was diagnosed with late-stage lung cancer.

An elderly woman with lung cancer is unlikely to have only lung issues alone. It's not an easy journey for both my mum and myself. It's not about how much mum has provided for me, but the difficult life versus death decisions a family caregiver like me is often tasked to take. While it is true that as a caregiver who lived with mum, I know best what mum likes or does not like.

A medical-based power of attorney is never stress-free nor straightforward. Daily journeys to work at 5 am, work for 8 hours, rush to clinic, hospital, or nursing home after dinner at 7 - 8 pm; waking up at 2-3 am to attend to the needs is highly demanding, physically, emotionally, and mentally. At the hospital, there is a group of doctors to speak with based on the individual's specific conditions. Then there is a nutrition expert who will rely on family member decisions. On top of this, there will be a post-treatment care program that the family member will need to decide on. And when a recommendation to the nursing home came from the doctor, the same set of various representatives from different aspects of her care will go to you for decision-making. The physiotherapist, the rounds doctor, the nurses, and so on. I wonder why there are no single points of contact who can be assigned to help solo caregivers.

My message for those caring for a sick elderly: Accept that the events will worsen. Secure whatever help, physical, mental, emotional, or spiritual regardless, any form that you can get hold of. You will need all and every single drop of it! Most do not understand or can imagine the strain and pressure of staying with a very ill parent. Siblings who visit will make mum happy for the moment. Their visit or appearance creates a moment of temporary relief for mum. Once the siblings left for their home, mum reverted back to the torment of her ailing body. This reality is something unseen by those who have no experience providing eldercare at home, and unless they are the ones providing the care, they do not understand.

Don't ever "shoot" the messenger! Don't ever utter a single harsh word to a sister or brother caring for a sick parent. You could drive them suicidal! Do not underestimate the pressures of elderly care.

Taking Singapore, as an example – medical costs have risen sharply, together with a greying population. Elderly care naturally falls on the dwindling community in their fifties or sixties. Folks within these age brackets are also facing job insecurities due to concurrent economic and pandemic crises. There have been no strong social structures in place to support sole caregivers who are typically single or childless couples.

Training of domestic helpers was done on a group basis. Each elderly's needs and family situation were highly unique. No two elderly would share the same combination of medical issues. With smaller and satellite family units, there needs to be stronger and affordable support networks for the caregiver.

My mum started with chronic indigestion problem when she was 81-years-old. Before this, she had been very active, getting out to have a walk around town, meet friends, take care of housework, re-do some of my housework (she felt that I am not clean or tidy enough sometimes), etc. The health journey from her 60's to 70's is relatively less complicated with minor ailments. However, her illness in her 80's was so bad she frequently had to visit the A and E to help her with the chronic problem. When TCM (Traditional Chinese Medicine) finally balanced her body digestive system, she suffered a bad fall in her bedroom upon getting up at 3 am one morning for the bathroom. She had a right hip fracture, which needed surgery that led to severe delirium at the hospital. She was then 84-years-old and, at that time, mistook my husband's hand as a cauliflower. She also kept telling me there were cabbages beneath her hospital bed. I was in complete shock. The diagnosis was a growth in her left lung suspected to be a tumour that had metastasized in her bone and early-stage dementia.

She subsequently develop more medical complication, which resulted in another hospital stay in less than a month. Later in the same year, she fell again in her bedroom while getting out of bed, trying to head for the bathroom. At that time, we had a helper taking care of her and sleeping in the same room. Mum had quietly moved out of bed, and no one in the house noticed till she dropped onto the floor with a bang coming from the fall of her walking stick. At this point, we had a diagnosis that mum had late-stage lung cancer with a small crack in one of her ribs, along with hollow spaces in both thigh and leg bones.

Due to her underlying cytopenic and atrial fibrillation conditions, there were severe risks of operations of any sort. She was highly prone to strokes and may not survive the anaesthesia necessary for orthopedic surgery nor a lung biopsy. Having cytopenia meant mum's bone marrow is no longer producing sufficient blood cells for her body. At the same time, she could not continue the blood-thinning medication for her atrial fibrillation. Shortly after her left hip fracture, she suffered several bouts of shortness of breath, requiring an oxygen concentrator. Within the same month, she had a massive right brain stroke rendering the left side of her body immobile.

The nursing home doctor and staff nurse felt that it would have been worse if she underwent a lung biopsy or any procedure requiring anesthesia. Within two weeks, her stroke progressed, her hands and feet became swollen, she was unable to speak, her chest became congested with pulmonary fluids, she lost a couple of her top canine teeth, started bleeding from the gums, and then spitting up blood. She went from breathing every now and then to continuously being under the oxygen concentrator for two weeks.

Let's pray mum's journey will be comfortable, and everything works out the way she wanted.

About May Quan Ho

May Quan Ho is a Product Stewardship and Regulatory Affairs (PS & RA) manager in a chemical industry. She has fifteen years of experience in the product regulatory and international trade compliance.

May's early career years were spent in various laboratory and technical management roles. Prior to transitioning into regulatory compliance, she had worked in sales and marketing support.

May holds a Ph.D. in Environmental Chemistry from the National University of Singapore. She enjoys writing and is passionate about sharing her experiences to inspire and help others.

https://www.facebook.com/may.q.ho

LOVE IN TIMES OF COVID

By Meenu Agrawal

"In every crisis, doubt or confusion, take the higher path - the path of compassion, courage, understanding, and love." Amit Ray

The year 2020 will be remembered for a long time, a period of time unprecedented in many ways. A timeline that not just marked the beginning of a new decade but unleashed the largest humanitarian crisis. I am like many others, a witness to the air of despondence and in the grips of negativity. Adding to this, I had to bear the loss of the untimely demise of my brother. Yet, I chose to look for the positives and hence this expression when I found loves triumphs at ordinary interludes of life and times in India.

"Crises and deadlocks when they occur, have at least this advantage that they force us to think." Jawaharlal Nehru

While there was every reason to choose despair, I thought, and I chose to see love. Love endures the most formidable challenges and trials of life. Love triumphs when it is easier to fall for hate and resentment. This is a story about two kids, a mother, and a dog set in the dense urban milieu of Maximum City, Amchi Mumbai. The protagonists are dwellers at the Middle Income Group Government Apartment Complex at Bandra East. Summer was about to blaze, and the last pleasantness of the winter air blowing across the apartment complex in a mid-February sunny season was oblivious to the perils in store.

Bandra East was a bustling place. A mix of Maharashtrian, Punjabi, and South Indian as well as an Anglo-Indian society. The cricket-crazy nation had an important location in the colony in the form of the MIG Club. Many street food hawkers were vending a variety of gastronomic delights to the residents. The colony was a 15-minute walk to perhaps the busiest central business district in Asia after Shanghai; The Bandra Kurla Complex.

Many residents at the complex had converted their flats into paying guest apartments. The young working professionals from the Financial District rented a place to stay close to work. Divya Chandra was a twenty-something analytics professional who had come to Mumbai from Hyderabad. She was smart, gorgeous, all-toned Zumba, and aerobic indulging, young, zippy, peppy, glib-talking urban chick. Her outward attitude & enthusiasm concealed her childhood struggles of enduring an alcoholic father & poverty. Ever since she escaped the tyranny at her home, she created this new world of liberation. She missed home, yet here in the colony, she had many street dogs that she took care of daily by feeding them milk, treats, and dinner. Every time she walks up to her paying guest apartment from work, or before her morning visits to the gym, these lovely animals will gleefully wag the tails and greet her.

Unmindful of the dirt on the street dogs, she would kneel and pet the pooches while talking to them as if they understood her language.

"Are you hungry Whitey," she would say, and the dog would stretch and bark as if saying yes. She would feed them small pieces of cheese that these pets love.

Iqbal, the corner store butcher, would save some bones and chicken wings and neck that she would collect. Divya would then steam and cook them; a quantity large enough to feed five dogs.

The kids in the neighborhood, David DeCosta, an aspiring college going lad and wannabe be cricket superstar, spent most of the time knocking the cricket ball at the nets at MIG. He, along with a few kids, would come by and chat with Divya. The kid and the girl had a flirty relationship.

The children had another friendly acquaintance. Fellow resident and walker Amar Deshpande, a 55-year-old bachelor, would pass by the kids and greet them, saying "Good job kiddos, the people who love animals cannot be bad people," he would murmur and then walk on. "I will send you a poem on Kala Nagar Residents WhatsApp group."

Even though he was three decades older, he had the uncanny ability to think young. His wearing of a young heart at his sleeve endeared him to the teenagers at the colony.

Ganpat, a 45-year-old bloke, was the watchman of Divya's apartments. He hated the dogs as they would overturn the garbage bins at night in search of food. This caused him more work. He used to have a 6-foot-long, one-inch-thick wooden stick. A night he would walk stealthy and hurl the cane aimed at the feet of the dogs. A wailing noise of the dogs would wake up the kid in the colony. They would come out to the balcony and reprimand the watchman. Whitey, the favorite of Divya, was carrying puppies, and she feared that the dog could not run from the stick thrown at her. She used to get nightmares thinking about the same.

Roselyn DeCosta, was a God-fearing mother who would prepare sumptuous shepherd stew for   the colony kids on Sunday. Ryan DeCosta was a strict college principal and a connoisseur of single malt and blues. Roselyn and Ryan were proud of their son David & wanted to support him in all his endeavors. Their methods were as different as chalk and cheese. The mother used love, whereas his father insisted on hyper-strict discipline, which resulted in constant quarreling.

Between the son, father, and mother. Neighbors were used to the high-decibel, hyperventilating screams on most weekends from the house of the DeCostas.

Trump was visiting India, and a lot of foreign visitors were expected for a grand roadshow at Gujarat, a reciprocal fanfare after the 'Howdy Modi' event at Huston a year ago. The news wires on air were already reporting a rare pandemic that was causing quite a scare, yet the reporters on CNBC were shirking the news off, saying that like in the care of H1NI Virus, SARS & MARS, that COVID 19 will be a passing cloud also.

India was gearing for a massive reception to the Presidential couple, and Ivanka and entourage were already here at Gujarat's Dolera. Over 200,000 people were expected to come. At a time when nations around the globe were shutting down borders, here were two nations going on with business as usual.

In the following week's news from Italy, Wuhan spooked the world as the pandemic began to cause unfrequented havoc and panic. The government in India swung into quick action and called for a draconian total lockdown, giving citizens barely 6 hours' notice.

The morning after the lockdown, the streets were desolate, and the street vendors vanished; shops, offices, and schools shut down. Everybody was afraid to come out of their homes. The WhatsApp groups were buzzing with the death toll, and everyone was watching the Johns Hopkins Pandemic update on an hourly basis.

Divya was looking for her favorite stray for two days. The other four dogs were in attendance except for Whitey. She sent a WhatsApp message with the pic of 'Whitey Missing' as well as posted it on Facebook and Instagram. Since there was a police patrol, no one dared to venture out. Amar Deshpande was always rebellious; he took his morning and evening walks wearing his N95 mask. He would look for milk vendors and bring milk to Divya's PG.

That morning, Divya was crying when Amar reached her flat. She was weeping like a kid as she feared that someone might have killed pregnant Whitey. Summer was peaking, and then the dogs would be thirsty.

Amar quickly organized a bunch of boys and scooted around the colony, searching for Whitey. David was keen to help, and he could not see Divya crying. Divya's mom from Hyderabad called Roselyn as she sensed something was wrong with Divya, and she was not picking up her calls. No posts on Insta or FB meant something is amiss. In the modern age, social media was a window to the teenager's mind.

Divya received a WhatsApp message from Amar at 3 am, as the incoming message reduced the volume of the Ariana Grande Spotify track. Old man had sent her his poem!

Kindness to Animals

Little children, never give
Pain to things that feel and live.
Never hurt the timid hare
Peeping from her grass green lair
Let her come and sport and play
On the lawn at close of day
The little lark goes soaring high
To the bright windows of the sky,
Singing as if there always spring.
And fluttering on an untried wing
Oh, let him sing his happy song,
Nor do these gentle creatures wrong

Ping! Another WhatsApp text with a video that was hardly visible but had sounds of squirming pups. In a flash, Divya called Amar and asked, "Where did you find her, I want to go there now."

A happy Amar told that her that he found Whitey with her litter of 4 pups under Nimbalkar Uncle's car. Nimbalkar was a retired school teacher, and his dusty Maruti Suzuki was hardly used for years, so Whitey found it a safe place to sneak in and litter.

Divya swung   her refrigerator door open, took a milk packet and some bread, and ran toward Nimbalkar Un-cle's   car. The streets were barren, and the night was eerie. The moment she reached the car, she called out for

Whitey. Out she came, wagging her tail. She hugged the pet and kissed her as her eyes were crying tears of joy. Whitey immediately started lapping the bowl of milk.

Divya texted the boys and had a plan to keep Whitey and the pups away from Ganpat's watchman and his wrath. There was no response from anyone. Divya thanked Amar. Before leaving the car, she placed a bowl of fresh water.

At about 7 am, Divya's phone rang; it was David. He was saying, "I am happy for you, sweetheart. I will arrange the stable that we usually use for the Christmas decoration atop their terrace." Within the next few hours, they moved the pups to the terrace. Amar offered to give the kids some money to make arrangements.

Months passed, and there was no sign of the lockdown relaxing; the infection count was rapidly rising, and the U.S. was leading with the number of cases. Visuals of New York was like an open medical emergency center.

Back home, the boys were getting frustrated about being indoors. They were hooked on the PUBG app. The gaming addiction was having a lot of ill effects on teens. The game is extremely violent; playing too much PUBG could make the kid less productive and edgy, disturbs sleep patterns & impairs physical and social wellness.

No cricket meant bottled up frustrations. The government had decided to open the liquor shops. During the lockdown, there were several cases of domestic violence, and the house of DeCostas was affected. David was very troubled.

News in times of crisis comes from all directions, particularly the negative ones. A famous Bollywood actor was found hanging in his apartment. There was an outpouring of grief, and a judgmental public started vile narratives of nepotism, drugs, and depression. Social media is a great connectivity platform, but the double-edged sword that it is, it amplifies negative news as well. Few threads become acerbic.

The boys and girls were actively texting about depression and despair that drove the actor to give it all up; some suspected murder. Amar would scold the kids for succumbing to news of poor taste and chide them often. He was an optimist, and he always encouraged people to see life as a glass half full. He was also a romantic who believed that love could heal most wounds.

All four of Whitey's pups survived. Now 4-months-old, they were running around the streets with carefree abandon. No traffic means less risk. Divya was regularly feeding the pets and a resident local veterinarian, Dr. Kadambari, treated the pups and dogs pro bono. Amar's money was used to buy rabies vaccinations and deworming medicines.

It was a rainy evening; David, Divya, and Amar teamed up for a long walk target of 15,000 steps by Bandra Band Stand. Vada Paw vendors were serving with masks, and at the end of the walk, it was a guilty pleasure to indulge in the spicy, oily snacking.

There was an incessant drizzle that made the roads slushy. As they reached their destination, they saw a huddle of boys around what seemingly a dog was hit by a stick. Divya ran and was aghast that one of Whiteys pups was hacked on the head. The puppy was whimpering; its mouth was bleeding; it was barely 4 months old. She broke down. David speed-dialed Dr. Kadambari. The boys were seething in rage as they suspected Ganpat.

No one could touch the pup because when someone neared, the pup wailed with a sharp shrill, it was in deep pain. From a distance, Divya could see Whitey, uneasy with sad eyes. Dr. Kadambari arrived and asked the boys to put a small muzzle around the pup's mouth. The mouth was oozing sticky blood, and the boys reluctantly held the dog by force. Divya could not bear the cries of the pup and ran to her flat sobbing. Dr. Kadambari administered a pain killer and some medicines. She instructed the kids to bring the pup to the clinic. The pup stopped wailing and had a twinkle in her eyes with a wag of her tail after she received her shot.

The treatment plan was to put the tender pup on drips. News reached Divya as Amar consoled her. He has bought a crate of beer and invited the boys to his flat and insisted that Divya came along. There was a sense of relief, and everyone was silently sipping their beer. Amar has fried some Bombil Fish and made some Kokam Curry. David offered to bring mutton stew and tempered lentils that his mom Roselyn had prepared.

Watching streaming series was a pastime when they met at Amar's home. Amar had eclectic tastes, and he has recommended that the gang tuned into Martin Scorsese's 'The Irishman.' Amar was a big fan of Robert De Niro, Al Pacino, and Joe Pesci. The crate of beer soon vanished as did the fish fry. The movie was a dark gangster drama.

The folks wanted more, Divya was on red wine, and the boys and Amar shifted to Old Monk rum. Divya observed that David was kind of edgy since the lockdown. She asked Amar to make David open up. David was putting up cryptic WhatsApp and Instagram posts lately. His Twitter posts were inundated with retweets on the suicide of the Bollywood actor.

Suddenly, David broke down. He was weeping about the deep depression that he was in for the past year. His not so impressive academic performance, the politics in cricket based on nepotism that favored rich dad's kid, the ban on PUBG, and the domestic violence at his home all contributed   to his depression.

Besides, he has seen Divya post a few messages on Instagram about a new relationship with her office friend. All were shocked; Amar and Divya thought that David was only casually flirtatious. Divya was a good 4-years older than David. When Amar spoke about all of them being good friends, and they will help David come out of his depression, David was irritated. He was high; he shouted at Amar, stating that he was an immoral man who had wrong intentions with Divya.

The moment David uttered that statement, Divya poured her glass of wine on David's face and slapped him. He started screaming, "You bitch..." Suddenly the room was like a keg with explosives about to be lit. Amar asked Divya to calm down. David got up in haste and ran away. Divya was sobbing. She was saying that she saw David as a good friend, and she has a wonderful relationship with Uncle Ryan and Aunty Roselyn. Roselyn was like a mother to her. She profusely apologized to Amar, and they called it a day.

In the afternoon the next day, there was a high-pitched cry from the DeCostas house. It was not the typical hyper-ventilated argument. People ran in to see David, pale blue, lying on the floor. Amar and Divya rushed in to call an ambulance. Roselyn was crying, Ryan was too. Ryan seemed   to have reprimanded David for coming home drunk, and David was still under the influence of the excessive beer when he woke up late for breakfast at 11 am. Soon afterward, he shut himself inside his room. There was a big thud of a chair falling, and suspecting something wrong, Ryan broke into David's room where he found his son hanging.

For a mother, her greatest hope is her son. She was sitting outside the ICU with a rosary in her hand. Sitting beside her was Ryan, reading the bible. Before that, there was a police case registered and formalities of which Amar was overseeing. It was a case of a partial hanging and a severe condition of asphyxiation. Amar's speedy response possibly saved the boy's life. Thankfully the doctor's report ruled out cerebral hypoxia and a cervical spine fracture.

Divya and Roselyn could see David through the glass as he was put on a respiratory ventilator. Doctors have advised a 48-hour observation. Amar received a text from Dr. Kadambari that Whitey's pup has fully recovered and was able to chew soft food; he was active and bouncing around. Amar called Divya aside and shared the text. Reading the text brought a smile to Divya's face.

Amar drove Ryan and Roselyn with Divya to the Mount Mary Church. They wanted to light a few candles and pray for David.

Things around the city were improving. Though Mumbai was the worst hit by the pandemic, her people's spirit was winning over a crisis yet again. Though there was a sharp rise in the infected, the recovery rate was rapid and encouraging. The state has admirably swung into action with makeshift ICU's to treat extreme cases.

Back at Kala Nagar, things were returning back to normal. The street hawkers and tea vendors were back on the street wearing masks, yet doing their job of feeding the people. Divya was pleased to see the puppy back on its feet bouncing. The group of residents during the monthly meeting called in Ganpat and advised him to restrain his cruelty. Ganpat was moved; he was expecting others to fire him; instead, the residents offered him financial help and spoke softly. Ganpat confided that when he saw how Divya grieved for the innocent pup, his heart melted, and he introspected as to why he was so cruel when he saw a young girl full of love and compassion to an animal.

David was discharged from the hospital. David had realized how much his parents loved him, and he was ashamed of the immaturity on his part to think of Divya and Amar. Roselyn told about the wonderful gesture of his friends and that he owed his life to a mentor and friend like Amar. Divya showed a video from her phone of a bouncy Whitey Junior.

At the church, Ryan was counseled by the Father. His streak of domestic violence was traced to his unrealistic disciplinarian excesses. He was advised to let go. Ryan had witnessed how Divya cared for the innocent animals and Amar's penchant for social service. Amar's ability to bond with kids several years younger was a lesson for Ryan.

As we age, it is our initiative that keeps us relevant to society. Our ability to care for beings, compassion, kindness, and understanding emanates from a deep capacity of love that all of us, as sentient beings, are capable of representing. Sticking together as a group, connecting with empathy and integrity, and a dose of selfless love brings about miraculous results.

Amar, Ryan, Roselyn, David, Divya, Ganpat, and their experiences through the worst pandemic isn't unique to them. When there is despair, hope lifts the spirits. Love has a natural capacity. Do not misunderstand love with other dynamics. Love is Pure – A Life Force. Love Prevails over any crisis. Love is understanding; Love is compassion, Love is friendship, Love forgives, Love never gives up. Love is humane! Each one of us is designed for a capacity of limitless love.

David was able to freely breath, Ryan an improved man, Divya made peace with her Dad, Amar kept his tryst with being a generous social service agent of camaraderie. Ganpat became the guardian of the strays. The world hasn't yet conquered the COVID 19 crisis, but the hopes of people around the planet have never been higher. Doctors, nurses, and public administrators heeded not just to their call of duty, but to a commitment that is a higher order of magnitude. To them, it was an opportunity to be of service to humanity at a time of crisis. They served with love and compassion. Soon will there be a day when the world would have won its battle with COVID 19. The battle with polio started in 1978, and victory was achieved in 2014.

We hope that the victory over COVID 19 is sooner and just around the corner. Until then, love will save the way. Love will continue to save everyone every day. Keep the faith and love with no limits. Love is a limitless capacity that all humans are naturally blessed with in abundance.

About Meenu Agrawal

Meenu is kind and very hard to find. She is someone who would settle for little joy in life rather than materialistic satisfaction. For her integrity reveals beauty so she does what is right even when you disagree with her. she doesn't care if you hate her guts or her views..

Her symbols being that of a MOMMY awesome, a corporate executive, runner, golf player, speaker, author, story teller, social worker. She needs to venture to the far corners of the planet and need to know the culture and life outside India. Her ambition is to be an inspiring leader and a responsible stakeholder in the society. She is a trusted friend and a beautiful soul to connect.

She believes in the quote " To be kind is more important than to be right. Many times, what people need is NOT a brilliant mind that speaks but a SPECIAL HEART that LISTENS"

Twitter - @Mintz05

Linkedin - Linkedin.com/in/meenu-agrawal-2507815

MY JOURNEY

By Monika Khanna

"When life gave me lemons, I chose to use them to add a whole lot of freshness!"

In this honest and revealing article, I share my domestic abuse journey, my need to forgive others and myself, and my transformed life. Today I am a mental and emotional resilience-building mentor to those who have been where I have been. It's these stories that give us hope and remind us ... there is always Light, and it's nestled within us ... we only need to spark it.

I am a 48-year-old single parent to three wonderful adults. An Executive Assistant and Business Resiliency Coordinator by profession, I work for a US MNC in Gurgaon. The profile entails an eye for details, out-of-the-box thinking, sagacity on the org environment's pulse, and an understanding of the pulse of the 5000+ workforce we have. The constant people interaction and their erratic behavioral patterns fascinated me, combined, of course, by my own personal struggles. The course on Neurolinguistics was a step toward formalizing my education into this fascinating world of human behavior. After the course, I offered my services as s a Sensei and Lead Facilitator for the support groups in the organization I currently serve. In these groups maintaining anonymity, we encourage open dialogue & help others and self through stories. It's a platform for colleagues who want to:

- Talk about any event that could be potentially causing them stress, anxiety, panic, depression, irritability, and the biggest foe of all, loneliness.
- Be a part of a place to talk about what's on your mind and in your heart.

I desire to spend my upcoming years practicing and offering support as a Life Coach and Counselor and reach out to mitigate emotional issues.

My childhood was, by and large, a simple one. Father was always away in different remote locations for work, while my mother stayed on in the city to ensure our education wasn't compromised. I grew up with an elder sibling who was the black sheep of the family. I had to take over the household's responsibilities early on in life as my father was away, and my sister wasn't available to shoulder these duties.

During my growing up years, I had only a couple of wishes, as many youngsters would have had back then ... to have a decent education/employment and treasure a decent, caring life partner and family. As a meritorious student, I studied on scholarships throughout and dreamt of having a decent job, post-education. With these rosy dreams, years flew by, and while I was in the second year of college, my maternal aunt introduced us to my ex's family, who were related to her through her husband's side, and proposed the alliance. Within three months of this initial interaction, I was married!!

I had grown up in a Mills & Boons romance where the partner was always loving, caring, and supportive, and life was always "happily ever after." I entered an arranged marriage with these dreams and moved to a new city, a new house, and a new family. John Lennon wrote a song with these words "Life is what happens to you while you are busy making other plans," and so it was for me.

Hmm ... Guess there were red flags right from the word go. Both of us were too young and naïve, I was barely 19, and he was 21-years-old. There was never an emotional connection. It was all for the family. We barely socialized, and the few interactions were limited to family. Don't recall having any "couples" time. There was no going out for ice-creams, movies, or outings. With the absence of emotional bonding, I was already doubting myself and feeling inadequate.

Every day seemed a struggle and not right. My inability to complete my studies, lack of contact with friends, and a feeling of isolation were the first signs of suffocation. And then began the subtle abuse!! Initially, it was in the form of gaslighting. "You don't know types – You are not under-standing – I don't want to do this, but you are forcing me to," was what I heard. Then began the sexual abuse. I was verbally assaulted and made to feel incapable of being a woman. It was difficult to feel happy with so much turmoil within it, and his touch made me cringe. I dreaded times alone with him.

My spouse, a businessperson, turned into an alcoholic and a womanizer. The business dwindled, and monies were lost. I picked up jobs to support myself. Gradually things worsened; I became the victim of domestic violence and abuse. When faced with debts and scarcity of money, he found recourse in hitting his parents and extorting money. Often, when I tried to intervene, I would be caught amidst the antagonism and get battered too. Initially, it was shoving and pushing. Later, it graduated to physical assault. Every evening was a nightmare when we dreaded his coming home drunk and thrashing us, abusing us, throwing tantrums, or breaking up things. My children were petrified, and I could see the emotional trauma they were going through. Their performance at school dropped, and they became socially withdrawn.

I tried speaking to my parents, my in-laws (with whom I was living with), and who were there every day to witness the abuse, and the extended family knew as well. All preached that things would be okay; it would   phase out. He is immature; you should chill. Try to understand him.

It didn't bother my spouse that people around him knew. He always played the victim card.

I felt all alone in many ways without real, meaningful support from my elders. I felt abandoned by the very people I trusted!

Any effort I made to wean my spouse off alcohol and desist from being violent against me did not work. Incidentally, the violence increased to a level where my husband tried to strangle me. I often saw a glimpse of glee when I begged to be spared as he attempted to suffocate me with all his might. His family was of no help in this matter, either. Even though I was ready to separate from him and still looked after my in-laws in a final effort to salvage the situation, they remained silent.

After 14 years of trying to salvage my marriage, I ran away from home with my children. I left all my possessions behind. I was forced to take this step as the violence was now percolating to the children. Both my children were witness to this behavior every night. They saw the grandparents and their mother being abused and threatened. The worst moments in the relationship were when I realized my children were showing signs of being socially withdrawn and quiet, academically suffering, and always scared. The **final act or situation that gave me the courage to speak up about it was** when he tried to hang me on the ceiling fan; I knew it was time. It hit me that no one would care if I died tomorrow, and the only sufferers would be my children.

The thought of my son possibly following in the same footsteps as his father or my daughter being abused, left me stunned. I could not be that example of helplessness. I had to do it for US.

I left my matrimonial   home and decided to start anew. My ex then tried to reach out on sympathy grounds. Then came fresh challenges. Seeking help wasn't easy at all. The parents were reluctant, and the extended family kept mum.

Nevertheless, I was firm I had to move out. I actually took refuge with a relative in another city for three months. After that, I relocated with some help from my parents and started a new life from scratch. My spouse never felt remorse at losing the children and me, nor did he try to help financially or emotionally. Even as I fought a bitter divorce, he troubled me all through the divorce proceedings. However, determined to give my children a better future, I kept going to help my children realize their dreams while preparing them for the vicissitudes of life.

CARPE DIEM … SEIZE THE MOMENT … TAKE A CHANCE, SOMETIMES LIFE GETS BETTER WHEN YOU TAKE A CALCULATED RISK. HAVE FAITH AND CONFIDENCE IN YOURSELF AND YOUR ABILITIES; IT MAKES A WORLD OF DIFFERENCE.

I needed a tremendous amount of healing to get over the battering experiences of my life. I tried meditation, reading, and talking to faith healers along with many other things, all of which helped me slowly get over the traumas

I faced. Being sexually abused left me scarred deeply and emotionally destroyed.

I have had my share of "Me Too" experiences during my work career, some of which have been very distasteful. All through this, I have been fortunate to have the support of a few people. My children and mother were a solid source of support through some of these travails.

With the long term emotional and mental repercussions of an abusive relationship, the trauma cannot be explained. The emotional scars never heal. You have to deal with depression and physical hate of self, as in my case, because I was sexually abused, too. Being in this TOXIC environment, you lose self-confidence, and your self-esteem is non-existent. I needed a tremendous amount of healing to get over the battering experiences of my life.

What keeps you wordless and carry on with that miserable life is fear of retaliation, social fear from family, loss of identity, and self-respect. It became an honor issue with my family; their morality was threatened if I spoke up, threats were constant, and the fear of failure was prominently highlighted.

Having been through all this, I still believe genuine love and respect are waiting for me. I strongly believe in marriage as an institution. That one abusive relationship does not define me.

Is there anything that I wish I had done earlier? I wish the people around me had recognized that I was a victim and in need of help. Often the victim is not able to realize the same and speak up for various psychological reasons. Any help at this stage or a person to talk to, share, discuss, or handhold can make the difference.

Right now, speaking about all this, I would advise victims currently suffering at the hands of domestic violence – Take YOUR time. Stand up for yourself. It won't make you argumentative. Sharing your feelings doesn't make you oversensitive. Saying no doesn't make you uncaring or selfish. If someone doesn't respect your boundaries and needs, it's them, not YOU; Speak up. There is support around; you just need to reach out.

Moreover, as you pick up the threads of your life again – Forgive yourself for not knowing better. Most importantly, **Forgive yourself for the survival patterns and traits you picked up while enduring trauma. Forgive yourself for being who you needed to be. It's not okay to say it's okay!!**

****

About Monika Khanna

Monika is an Executive Assistant & Business Resiliency Co-ordinator by profession. A single parent to three wonderful adults, she is also a lead facilitator for various Support groups where maintaining anonymity they encourage open dialogue & enlighten others and self through stories. The constant interaction with people and their erratic behavioral patterns fascinate her, combined of course by her own personal experiences and journey towards light. Having survived domestic abuse, she is on a path to encourage others like her to speak up, and shares her thoughts to show people that they are not alone. https://youtu.be/F9XpO-5qsZE

She desires to spend her approaching years practicing and offering support as a Life coach & Counselor and reach out to mitigate emotional issues.

https://www.facebook.com/monica.khanna.1610

https://instagram.com/monicaakhanna?igshid=p0sbf0zu511k

https://www.linkedin.com/in/monika-k-b80803b

PARABLE OF KID

By Ho Ee Kid

It was a stormy night. Sitting all alone in the balcony of my HDB flat, I stared at the flashes of thunder in the faraway skies. In my hands, a stack of bills. It just felt like the whole world had come crashing down on me. All because of a virus called COVID19, too tiny for the naked eye to see. Twenty years of hard work, twenty years of blood & sweat are in danger of disintegrating right before my eyes. Customers are canceling orders; my debtors are defaulting, my suppliers hounding me for payment. What have I done wrong? Just when things were looking up at the end of last year, this had to happen. Closing my tired eyes …

Why am I all dressed up in this strange clothing? I looked up and saw this familiar face, isn't that King Solomon? Where am I? Then I saw the King gesturing me over. As I moved closer, I heard him say, "Benaiah Yehoyada, you are one of my most trusted ministers. Therefore, I am entrusting you with this vital mission."

I bowed and replied, "Yes, my Sire, if it is within my power to do so."

The King continued, "There is a certain ring that I want you to bring to me. I wish to wear it for Pesach (Passover), which gives you about six months to find it."

"Your Sire, if this ring exists anywhere on this earth, I would surely find it and bring it to you. But what makes this ring so special?" I said.

"This ring has special powers. If a happy man were to look at it, he would become sad. And if a sad man looks at it, he would become happy."

I then knew what the King was trying to do. Knowing that this was an impossible task, he meant to humiliate me during the Pesach. I then set out on this impossible task to find this ring. I traveled the entire kingdom and asked every merchant and every jeweler in the cities I visited. None knew or had heard of such a ring. Soon Pesach was near. With a heavy heart, I made my way back to Jerusalem. On erev-Pesach (eve of Passover), I decided to take a stroll through the poor quarters of Jerusalem. I noticed a merchant selling odd pieces of jewelry spread out on a threadbare rug.

Out of desperation, I approached the merchant, "Would you, by any chance, have heard of this magic ring. It is so magical that the happy wearer will forget his joy, and the broken-hearted wearer forget his sorrows?"

The merchant looked at me silently for a while. He then reached out for a plain looking gold ring from the carpet. On this ring, he engraved יעבור זה גם and then passed it to me. When I read the words, my heart smiled. The next day, the entire city was celebrating the festival with great joy. I was in the palace, and all the King's ministers had gathered, each one waiting to have a good laugh over my predicament.

"Well, my old friend," King Solomon said. "Have you found what I have sent you to seek?"

Everyone laughed, and the King himself smiled. To everyone's surprise, I held up a small gold ring.

"Here it is, your Sire! The ring that you desired."

King Solomon took the ring in his hands and read the engraved words. The smile vanished from his face. On the ring were engraved the Hebrew letters 'Gam Zeh Ya'avor' (This Too Shall Pass). At that moment, King Solomon realized the meaning of impermanence, and that all his wisdom and wealth and power are but fleeting things. There will come a day when it too would all be nothing but dust.

Trrrrrriiiiiinggggggggg!!! I woke up to the sound of the alarm. It was undoubtedly a strange dream, but how real it felt. I could still remember all the details of the dream, right down to every conversation I had. Then it dawned on me.

Gam Zeh Ya'avor. Like all things in this world, nothing is permanent. Especially amid this pandemic, this phrase helped give me a much-needed perspective, humility, and strength to cope with what I am experiencing. However tough the situation might be right now, it too will soon come to pass. Nothing is permanent. It reminds me that when we are in good and happy times, we must remember to value what we have and live life to the fullest. A strange dream indeed, but it made me feel so much better. I feel all refreshed, ready to do battle again, knowing that there will come a day when this virus will pass.

In the next few weeks, I set about to sort my business issues with new vigor. Despite knowing that this crisis, too, will pass, it still wasn't fun facing each day as it was all about business survival. It was getting to the point that I dreaded waking up each day with nothing much to look forward to. And there was this really disastrous day. On that day, I found out in the morning that a long-time friend and customer had a heart attack and passed. His death hit me hard. He had been one of the loyal customers that was still supporting me. In addition, he still owed my company money. Then, in the afternoon, my staff had a big tiff with a customer and left the office in a huff. I had to call the customer to apologize and promised to send the things she ordered to her immediately. On my way to deliver, my car broke down. By the time I got the car towed to the workshop and took a taxi to deliver my customer's goods, it was close to midnight. When I got home, I crawled into bed …

Why am I walking barefoot in this deep bamboo forest? Hmm … I have on a yellow robe. Touching my head, I realized that I was a bald monk!!! It felt downright weird. Suddenly I heard a loud growl. Instinctively, I knew it was a tiger. I took a quick glance behind me and spotted this ferocious tiger racing toward me. I ran for dear life. I knew that if this goes on, the tiger will soon catch up to me. Suddenly, I screeched to a halt. I was standing right against the edge of this ominous looking cliff. And right at the bottom, I could see a river. With no time to lose, I grabbed hold of a vine growing by the side of the cliff and started climbing down. Up above, I could still hear the tiger roaring away. Halfway down the cliff, I took the opportunity to look down, and to my horror, I saw crocodiles with their jaws wide open, staring up at me. I was petrified. Looking up, I can still see the tiger snarling away. As I hung there, I noticed that just right above the vine that I was holding onto; there was a small hole on the side of the cliff.

I saw two noses emerging from the hole. It was two mice, one Black & one White. The two mice started gnawing away at the vine that I was holding onto. It certainly seems like my days are numbered. Suddenly, I spotted to my right a patch of green. It was a plant growing on the side of the cliff. To my delight, I spotted a fat, luscious, red wild strawberry growing from it. I stretched out my arm, plucked it, and popped it into my mouth. "How sweet this strawberry taste!!!" And then I felt my hands losing grip of the vine, and I was falling ...

Ouch!! My eyes opened, and I realized my face was looking at the floor. I must have fallen out of bed. That was certainly a weird dream. I can still feel that strawberry's sweetness in my mouth. I started recollecting the events in my dream. The tiger was chasing after me and me escaping from it. That represented something bad that had already happened. Hmm, so like my own past. It had been a tough struggle setting up my business. Somehow, I managed to survive, and we were turning the corner. Then there were these crocodiles, all waiting to eat me up. Since they are waiting, that means the incident had not happened yet. So that must be the future. I can identify with that. Even my business future looks pretty bleak. Then there is me holding onto the vine, that must be the present. Black and white mice? Perhaps they are Night and Day, and their gnawing away at the vine represents the constant passing of time.

What about the strawberry? I certainly did remember enjoying its sweetness, and for the moment, everything else is forgotten. That's it ... the strawberry represents all the little moments of joy and happiness that are happening all the time, provided I recognized it. Let me think back to yesterday. As I slowly recollect the day in more detail, I did remember as I was leaving the house, my beagle, Snoopy, came prancing to me, and I picked him up and gave him a big hug. At that point, I was thinking to myself, what a great way to start the day. Then there was the dinner I had after towing the car to the workshop. The owner treated me to a Nasi Lemak dinner. I was utterly blown away by the taste of the savory coconut rice, the yummy beef rendang, and the decadent spicy sambal. And that night, when I reached home, there was a tumbler of Hot Gingko Tea waiting for me with a little love note. I still recalled feeling fortunate that I have so many people who still loved me. Maybe that's the trick to managing life. It may be great to have a big victory, but life is not all about that. If we slowed down and looked around us, we can find many such strawberries to savor. Some may be small, some big, some sweet, and some sour. But who cares!!! They are strawberries to be savored, and each one is special.

From that day onward, the days became more enjoyable as I looked for things to appreciate. I appreciated waking up every morning, still feeling alive. I give thanks for good health, which is, in essence, true wealth. I enjoy every unexpected treat that a good friend chooses to surprise me with, and in return, I dish out surprise treats, and the look of appreciation on my friend's face is music to the heart. And when I realized that I look forward to cherishing such strawberries in whatever forms, more and more appeared, and it teaches me that every day is indeed a special day. I also look forward to dishing them out, knowing that what goes out would eventually come back to its owner many times over.

Of course, it was still a struggle keeping the business alive. Many times, I wonder if I'm doing the right thing to set up my own business and having to suffer its consequences. Maybe it would have been better if I had just worked for someone instead and draw a regular salary. One afternoon, I decided to go to the Changi beach to do some reflection. There were hard decisions to make, whether to close down the business or slog on, not knowing how long this pandemic would last. I found two coconut trees and strung up my hammock. I sink into the hammock, close my eyes, enjoy the calming sound of the breaking waves and the whisper of the cool breeze...

What is this strange place ... I looked up and realized that I am not alone. I could see another three people, all of them looking equally puzzled. We are all wearing a white shirt and pants. At least I am not alone. We introduced ourselves. There was Ahmad from Singapore who was a Grab delivery man. The last thing that he could remember was that he was delivering food on his motorbike, heard a loud bang, and then he found himself here. John is an Englishman. He remembered he was with his girlfriend, and they were getting it on in the hotel room when he felt severe chest pain. When he closed and opened his eyes, he was here. Malaysian Rajoo's tale was fascinating. He was out hunting in the oil palm plantation. He recalled someone shouting "Babi" (pig), a loud bang, and he was here. All I could remember was lying in the hammock and closing my eyes. It is what it is and certainly does not look like there is any way back to where we came from.

It was a strange land looking like some desert scene from Star Wars. As far as our eyes can see, there was nothing except a dirt path that just mysteriously appeared in front of us. Where does this path lead to? Since we were not going to achieve much by standing around, all four decided to follow the path. I was thinking to myself, "Will the four of us eventually split up and go our separate ways according to our personal beliefs." Finally, we came to a fork in the path, and far away, we can see what looked like mountain ranges. One path led to the left while the other to the right. We all stood there, wondering which path we should choose.

Suddenly an old man appeared. I have to admit he does look a little like Dumbledore.

He said, "Welcome, my friends. You will all soon be approaching your new home. I am here to guide you as much as I am permitted on how you can carry on. In front of you, see two paths. One of them leads to Heaven, a place more beautiful than you can ever imagine. The other path leads to Hell, a land full of darkness, despair, and wretched souls. All I can say is once you chose your path and reach your destination, you will not be able to turn back. My only advice is don't be frightened, for that reward you get in the end will be that which you deserve. So, go forth and choose your path. If you think you have led a just life, you will reap as you have sowed. You may now proceed on, one at a time and each must walk this path all by themself."

After saying this, the old man vanished into thin air.

All four of us looked at each other for a while. We were taken aback at this somewhat unorthodox way of getting to Heaven or Hell. Especially when this was not how we believed it was supposed to work. Finally, we decided that we must still proceed on. To decide on who to go first, we played scissors-paper-stone to determine which of us should go first.

John won and got the first opportunity to choose. He decided on the right path. The remainder of us three sat around to wait for some form of sign that the next one may proceed. After a while, we saw John coming back to us, and his face was pale. John told us that as he moved further down the path, he could hear fierce sounds of wild animals, the skies above him were all dark with ominous storm clouds, and the ground trembled every so often as he walked. He became more and more frightened and decided that the road to Heaven should not be so ominous-looking and decided to turn back.

John shared his experience with all three of us. Then John decided to try the left path instead. As he ventured forth on the left path, he, too, encountered various ominous signs that did not indicate that it was the path to Heaven. He kept worrying about how far he could go before he cannot turn back anymore. With each step, his feet felt heavier and heavier, and the fear in his heart grew and grew. Finally, he could not take it any longer and returned to the start point and share his story with all of us.

Seeing that John could not decide as to which path to take, Ahmad and myself suggested to Rajoo that he now take his turn. Rajoo, however, was too petrified after listening to John's stories. Neither path sounded correct.

"I'm going to think about it for a while. One of you go on first," Rajoo said

It was now Ahmad's turn.

"I'm picking the right-hand path, and I'm not turning back," he said.

We waited for a very long time, and suddenly we heard a loud booming voice say, "NEXT." I guess that's the sign for one of us to proceed.

It was now my turn to choose. John said he thought he heard a wild animal eating Ahmad, and a chill spread through us. Although I am not sure if I was making the right decision, I decided to choose the left path. Quietly I said to myself: "Come what may, whatever happens, I'll still go forward and make the best out of it."

As I proceeded on the path, things quickly went from bad to worse. There were horrific shrieks and growls from wild animals, the storm and hailstones lashed away at my face. The clouds raged with fierce thunderbolts, and the ground shook every time lightning struck nearby. Still, I proceeded on until I finally saw a sign that said, "HELL." Behind me, the path had disappeared, and there was no path of retreat.

Before me lies a dark and depressing place, forever wet, full of people living in run-down shelters. The people lived in constant fear of attacks from wild animals and roaming gangs that pillaged whatever they could lay their hands on. Everywhere I went, I was told that this was a land cursed by the devil and that things are going to get worse for all eternity.

I thought long and hard. "I promised myself that I would not retreat from this path and make the best of it. Hence, I refuse to listen to these voices of doom. Within myself, there is no hell, and my conscience is clear. So why should there be Hell on the outside?"

From that point on, I went forth in confidence and taught the people that they did not have to live in run-down shelters and that they could change their circumstances so that they would not have to live in fear. I also questioned their beliefs that the devil cursed the land. A handful of people took hope and listened, but the rest were afraid and even looked upon me as an enemy, fearing I would make things even worse than they were.

I gathered all the people who would listen, and there were few. But for those who listened, we refused to accept the place we were given as a final resting place. We began to make plans for beautiful new homes. The best land we could find was an island that lay in the middle of an unin-habited swamp. We built a bridge to reach it. We then drained the island and built our homes on it. We fenced up the island to protect it from gangs and wild animals. Bit-by-bit, we added beautiful gardens and farms. The gangs did not disturb us as we were all united in helping and pro-tecting each other. Soon, we started to adopt the wild an-imals who became friendly with the people who nurtured them. Somehow, as days pass, even the dark clouds and storms began to subside, and bright sunny days became a common sight.

The people who were against us saw what happened, and slowly they, too, took courage, and one-by-one other parts of Hell became transformed into beautiful homes, gardens, farms, and picturesque landscapes. After some time, there was nothing but beauty and peace in the whole of Hell. I surveyed the now beautiful land and came to a realization. There was one more thing that needed to be done. I walked to the original entrance and found the old sign, which said, "HELL." I tore it down and replaced it with one that said, "HEAVEN."

As I did so, another path with a fork appeared, and so did the old man. His look caught my eyes, and he said, "I think you know what you must do."

I looked back and said, "I see I must choose again.

"Correct," said the old man.

"Before I proceed, can you tell me the fate of John, Ahmad & Rajoo?" I asked.

"Ahmad is in a place that very much resembles the place that you have created. He has one regret, and that is he wishes that he had a part in creating the paradise where he lives. When the desire becomes strong enough, he will be given another path to choose and will wind up in a place called "Hell" as you did. And he will be given an opportunity to build Heaven. John and Rajoo are still paralyzed with fear, afraid to make a decision. They are the ones who are truly in Hell, yet sooner or later, they must choose and proceed onward," the old man answered.

"And what lies ahead for me?" I asked.

"The unknown," said the old man.

The statement sent shivers up my spine, and yet, I was glad at the same time. And with no hesitation, I proceeded on the path to the right and fell into a deep hole …

My mouth was in the sand. I must have fallen from the hammock. I stood up from the fall, and still in front of me was the sight of the blue sea. The sun is setting fast. Looking at my watch, I realize that I had slept for almost two hours, but it sure felt like a lifetime. What was that weird dream about? Slowly the lesson dawned on me. Heaven or Hell is a choice of what we make out of our life in the present. Like in the dream, I had chosen my path and accepted whatever life has thrown at me so far, and I have soldiered through it. So, why should I be discouraged just because there is another adversity in front of me now? Surely, compared to what I had just experienced in my dream, this is nothing. I came back from the dead, and for that, I am grateful. After all, I still have loyal clients, my faithful staff, and despite the short-term problems that I am facing, the business still has a lot of opportunities to grow. If I can build Heaven from Hell, I can certainly turn whatever adversity I am facing now into Heaven. With a renewed sense of confidence and purpose, I walked toward Changi Village hawker center to get myself the best nasi lemak in town.

1st story is a well-known story of King Solomon;

2nd story is a well-known Zen story.

Note: 3rd story adapted from "The Parable of Life" in The Immortal by JJ Dewey

About Ho Ee Kid

Kid lives in sunny Singapore where he lives life to the fullest. Always game for any adventure, this is what led him to taking up this challenge to write a chapter for this book, Kid is a jack-of-all-trades and masters of a couple. His interests are varied, ranging from leading curated adventure treks in Singapore, tea-tasting, tai-chi and investment. In addition, he loves to pen nrambling thoughts in his Facebook, which incidentally led him into this adventure of writing for a book. When Kid is in a more serious mode, he leads na group of like-minded professionals on a whirlwind wellness adventure that includes meridian therapy, aromatherapy & amp; anti-aging cell therapy. Kid's dream is to bring his Meridian101 and anti-aging wellness business to *various* countries all over the world and introducing more people into the world of natural wellness.

Connect to Kid on Facebook: *https://www.facebook.com/hoeekid*

Email: *hoeekid@yahoo.com*

FB Meridian101 Health Hack Group: *www.facebook.com/groups/607473640117279/*

FB Guasha Your Way To Good Health: *www.facebook.com/groups/865181593928795/*

FB LUV@ADVENTURE: *www.facebook.com/groups/102357963199140/*

FB LUV@SVASTHA : *www.facebook.com/groups/241449349622734/*

RACISM AND GRIT

By Dee Khanduja

I'm the daughter of Indian immigrants, born and raised in the UK. I grew up in a hostile, racist, and violent neighbourhood called Basingstoke. It was in this environment that I had my first taste of racial hate, bullying, and violence. It was a fight for survival.

It was also in this environment that I first started to develop my grit muscle.

I've been obsessed with understanding grit for over a decade. What is it? Are we born with it? Can we learn it? How do we become gritty?

I realised the reason I was able to survive a tough upbringing and grow to become a gritty 'action-taker' was that my childhood experiences had presented opportunities for me to practice igniting my own grit.

There are many definitions of what grit is. I like to describe grit as a state of mind where you are committed to getting things done and will take the necessary action despite the challenges.

I believe we all have a 'grit-muscle,' but it needs to be ignited and exercised to function. If we can be gritty about our dreams, they become our reality.

Allow me to share some clips from my childhood to hopefully show you that you, too, can get through tough moments if you learn to ignite your own grit.

Hate

My family owned a grocery shop in the UK, and we lived in a flat on top of it. Think grey/brown-toned, low-rise flats, housing families at the lower end of the socio-economic scale. Think of families on government benefits, think right-wing racist gangs, think drugs and alcohol, think violence, and think intimidation. More so, think white-supremacy, racist slurs graffitied on walls, think one-brown-family-caught-amongst-all-the-above, and breathe.

This was my home from the age of 3-13 years old.

Our shop sold everything from daily essentials like milk, bread, and eggs to frozen goods and pet food. My entrepreneurial parents would constantly try out different ideas to bring in more customers and create revenue streams.

They started video rentals, they brought in arcade machines to keep shoppers in the store for longer, and they even created an Indian food takeaway.

It was quite sadistic that the same punters who racially abused us in the day would then order my Mum's home-cooked food in the evening, only to smash our windows later in the night. This was not a one-off occurrence.

My folks were highly educated. Dad was a qualified Chemical Engineer who studied at Leeds University in the UK, and Mum was an international hockey player who represented India, as well as having a string of degrees to her name.

Soon after arriving in the UK around 1972, my Mum quickly discovered that a pile of poo was more noteworthy than her name, fame, and Indian degrees.

So, what are highly educated (yet rejected) immigrants with no support and very little money to do when trying to settle in a country that doesn't seem very welcoming?

Start a business, of course!

The birth of a business

Clearly, my folks didn't do enough due-diligence about the neighbourhood they chose to call home for a decade.

"Let's open a supermarket, sell essentials, and a mish-mash of other stuff, slap-bang opposite a pub full of drunkards in a super racist neighbourhood. Let's raise our three British-born, yet totally Indian-looking kids, in this wonderful welcoming country called England," said no one.

My folks ran our shop without any business experience, or tools and defences to deal with the daily hate. They would discover grit and resilience on the job, as would I.

Condoms and frozen peas

One day, as Mum went about restocking the frozen food section with pizzas, chips (and other crap processed frozen produce that the UK tends to love feeding its people), she discovered a deflated balloon.

Except it wasn't a balloon at all. It was a condom placed amongst the peas. A friendly welcoming gift from our kind neighbours.

The problem with finding condoms amongst frozen food is that it can be a game of 'hide and seek.' So frequent were the 'condom hiding' incidents that my parents would do a 'sweep' of the freezers to pick out the undesired foreign objects before the daytime trading would start.

The condom-planters became more creative over time and would shift their positioning so the soggy rubber could be found literally anywhere. Sometimes it was on the alcohol shelf; other times, it was amongst the eggs or the cakes or the tinned foods. Hiding objects amongst the tin food was genius since you could slot it behind the tins at the back, and they wouldn't be discovered until a customer eventually stumbled across them.

Thank goodness Google ratings and Facebook reviews didn't exist back then. I'd hate to think about how our little shop would have scored. Sometimes the condoms were unused and still shiny and new. Finding these condoms was a happy (and clean) moment. Other times, our friendly neighbours weren't so kind and would ensure they used the condoms first (presumably to get their monies worthwhile practicing safe sex). They would later deposit their bodily fluids in our freezer. I don't think the intention was to freeze their sperm literally.

Once they got so bored with their condom-planting tricks, they decided to bring their spermy remnants to our very front door and posted it through our letterbox ... without an envelope.

Intimidation

The punters we so desperately 'needed' as customers were usually busy drinking in the pub opposite our store. Others would hang around in gangs outside our shop, drinking cheap/free alcohol (free because it was often stolen from our shop during their frequent night-time raids, where they would smash our windows and help themselves to our stock).

Smashed Glass

The sound of smashed glass, followed by our screeching shop alarm, was a familiar sound to my little ears, and a signal that we had been robbed. Again. Every time our alarm sounded, I would jolt awake, heart-pounding, and reach for my inhaler as I struggled to breathe due to panic. I've had asthma since I was a child.

My innocent eyes would watch my parents swiftly change from their nightclothes, dash to the front door while instructing us to bolt and chain the door from the inside and not open it to anyone. My Mum trained us well on locking ourselves in our homes, hiding if anyone knocked on the door.

They would race down to our shop, our livelihood, to switch off the alarm. They'd then assess the damage, counting the loss in pounds, while silently crying over how much further debt the clean-up operation would create.

Childish questions

As a child, I remember thinking, 'Why do people hate me because I'm brown?'

'Why are they calling me a Paki?' (an insulting slur pointed at those of Pakistani descent, which ironically I'm not, but that's not the point.)

'Why are they smashing our windows? Why are they putting used condoms through our letterbox?'

'Why are they stealing from us? Why are they threatening my parents?'

'Why are they graffitiing racist slurs on our walls?'

'Why did they throw that brick through our lounge window while we were eating dinner?'

'Why do the gangs of kids chase and throw stones at my brother and me?'

'Why did they smash our car up and place an industrial-sized metal bin on the roof?'

Why do scary gangs stand outside our house, knocking on our door, and shouting through our letterbox?'

'Why do they say 'Go back to your own country,' when I'm from the UK?'

'Why do I have to lock myself in my own home? WHY?'

When fear grips...

When I became aware that my skin colour was the reason for the hate, I wanted to be white. I would try and scrub my brown skin off in the bathroom ... but the brown stayed, as did the racial hatred around us. All I wanted was for my family and me to feel safe. Shouldn't this be a fundamental human right?

Lioness

One day Mum was sitting alone on a bench opposite our shop. No one else was around. The gang leader, an intimidating skinhead with a scar across his face, came toward her. He was swinging an electric cable that had a plug attached to it, the kind that you use to plug a kettle or rice cooker to the wall.

He walked toward my Mother, provoking her with both racial and sexual slurs, telling her there was nowhere for her to run and hide and no one to protect her. He paced toward her, ready to attack with his weapon.

In an instant, Mum made a decision. She decided that no matter how much it would hurt to be lashed by his whip, even if she were to be struck in the face with the dangerous 3-prong plug at the end of his cable, she would stand up against him on this particular day.

She decided to use her grit to make a stand against racism and violence. That day, she was standing up for every person who had faced discrimination. She stood up for every woman who met with violence at the hands of a man. That day she was prepared to put herself in a dangerous position because she cared enough to make a stand.

She rose from her seated position, stared at the white skinhead in the eye, and told him she was "ready to take him on." She stood her ground.

The man hesitated, not expecting her to rise against him. He expected her to be meek, or to run away, or plead with him not to hurt her. He expected her to submit.

She did not.

As he came closer to her, now swinging the cable in full force to frighten her, Mum summoned her courage and became fearless. She dared him to try and come closer.

The next moment a random lady spotted the altercation from a distance and, sensing danger, shouted at the skinhead to STOP and threatened to call the police.

My Mum kept her eyes firmly fixed on the man and repeated, "I'm ready for you."

Whether it was the fact that Mum wasn't going down without a fight, or the interruption of the lady, or both, the gang-member ran off. When he was clearly out of sight, my Mum sat down, shaking and trembling, as the tears poured from her soul.

This incident turned out to be an important win for my family. This was the day the thug and his cronies realised we would no longer be silent.

Some may find my Mother's stance courageous, others stupid. But her logic was that she had to stand up toward the racial hatred. She knew if she continued to be intimidated, the torment would get worse. She also knew that she was raising three young children who were watching and modeling her behaviour. She was not prepared to model a subservient relationship with the ignorant white folk in our neighbourhood.

She chose to model grit and resilience when it came to matters she cared deeply about.

The Stone and Me

There was a local gang of kids led by a ringleader called Billy. They would torment my brother and I, chasing us, throwing stones, spitting at us, and calling us names. Anything to break us physically and mentally. Sometimes they succeeded (we were outnumbered), but one day they did not.

One day we had a stand-off with Billy and his gang. They started throwing stones at my brother and I. Stones and rocks were being hurled at us with speed. We dodged them as best as we could until one stone skimmed past my ear. It was dangerously close to my face.

I instinctively recoiled backward and fell. The gang, thinking they had hit their target, started cheering and jeering. It was at that   very moment rage erupted within me, and I made a decision. I became my Mother. A nine-year-old lioness.

Lioness Junior

I grabbed the closest stone and transferred all my anger, sadness, shame, and resentment into the rock. With zero fear in my stomach and a raging fire in my eyes, I sprinted toward the gang screaming my war cry.

For the first time, I took the fight to them instead of running away. I stretched my arm back and threw the stone with the might of an Olympic javelin thrower. I aimed squarely for Billy's face. I willed the stone to strike him. I wanted to hurt him as much as he had hurt us.

But I missed him.

My anger-stone ended up smashing a window of a nearby house. The sound of the smashed window was all too familiar to me. Although this time, it was not a window in my home that had been smashed.

For a few moments, there was silence and stillness as we all stood stunned. Then fear ran through my veins, and I reverted to being a scared nine-year-old again. The Lioness in me had shrunk to a mouse.

I began running as fast as I could, all the way home, away from the scene of the crime. The adrenaline and cortisol rushed through my body, bringing me the gift of speed. I ran home to my bedroom and hid under the blankets, quivering.

Thoughts started racing through my mind: "What had I done? I'm going to be in so much trouble. My parents are going to be so angry and disappointed. My parents can't afford to fix that person's window."

"Shall I stay quiet about it, or shall I own up? What should I do?"

The internal conflict raged within as I cried. I didn't mean to smash anyone's window, but I had had enough of being bullied for being brown. I felt the injustice, and it wasn't right nor fair. I had defended myself, yet I had made the problem worse.

Climax

There was a sharp knock on our front door. My heart pounded as I heard my Mother open the door to angry voices.

It turned out that the gang had reported me to the person who lived in the house with the smashed window. They delighted in accompanying the owner to my front door, so he could rage at the kid who damaged his property.

My Mother listened calmly as the owner of the house shouted at her about his window. She was experienced with the perils of dealing with broken glass, so she apologised to the man and explained that the council would fix his window without cost to him. He demanded to see me and wanted an apology from me, not my Mother   .

My Mother called me from my room. Not just to apologise, but so that I would have the opportunity to use my voice. I meekly made my way to her side and faced the angry man and the gang at close range. I felt physically sick. The earlier bravado had vanished, leaving me feeling exposed. Sensing my fear, Mum placed a reassuring hand on my shoulder.

My Mother asked me to apologise to the man, and I did so dutifully, and I meant it. After apologising, I went into a rant explaining why I had thrown the stone and how the gang threw stones first. My Mother   let me speak. She wanted me to own my voice.

The gang of kids erupted in rebuttals, eight voices drowning out one. My Mother   ordered everyone to let me speak or leave her property. She was creating the space for me to stand up for myself in the safety of her presence. And so I spoke, and to this day, I speak out when injustice is served my way.

Mum did not shout nor reprimand me as I had feared. Instead, she held me, kissed my forehead, and explained that hurt people … hurt people. That a bully is almost certainly broken themselves. With a wink and a smile in jest, she told me to aim better next time.

Igniting grit

What is the point of me sharing all this, and what has it got to do with grit?

Well, I've come to realise that igniting grit seems to have three ingredients that show up, not only in my own stories but all the gritty stories I have ever heard:

1) **Care** – You need to deeply, unapologetically care about the issue/cause/matter/subject to get gritty about it. If you don't care about it deep in your bones, you can't get gritty about it. What this means

is you are unlikely to stick to your goal, plan, or mission over the long run. So what do you truly care about?

2) **Decision** – When you care about something enough, you decide to act. It's your decision that changes the outcome. Gritty people make unshakeable decisions.

3) **Courage** – When you care about something deep enough to decide to take action, you can summon courage through your journey, or in the moments you need it.

Grit in Action

My Mum *cared* enough about the injustice of how we were treated to finally make the *decision* to stand up to the gang members. This required her to summon her *courage*, time and time again.

I *cared* about not letting kids bully me, then *decided* to stand up to the gang of kids, which required me to have *courage*.

For the reader

Gritty people are change-makers; they create companies, they fail and rise. Gritty people keep going and growing; they fight for injustice; they are survivors, and they are warriors.

Now, more than ever, we need more gritty people to rise and take their positions for the betterment of humanity overall.

It is my deepest hope that you can ignite your own grit about the things you deeply care about.

About Dee Khanduja

Dee Khanduja goes by the moniker The Gritty Girl. She is an International Speaker speaking about grit and courage, and champions causes related to the 'Rise of the Woman'.

At home she lives with her husband, 2 kids, a dog, 2 turtles and countless fish, whilst managing a community of mama-entrepreneurs to strive for heart-led growth.

Professionally, Dee writes for American Association magazine and Expat Living Magazine, as well as blogging on Medium. She is also penning her first book from a 4-part fantasy genre book series.

She has 20-years experience working in the recruitment sector in Europe and Asia, having owned her own employment agency for 14 years. She has also worked on start-up projects within the education, e-learning, and e-commerce, and legal-tech space.

As a Certified Futurist and Long Term Analyst™, Dee works with corporates and individuals to train and coach them around the 'Future of work', emerging career trends and career strategy.

Despite her multiple hats, her core message is for all of us to 'do the work' to discover our internal gifts, and share these with the rest of humanity.

LinkedIn

www.linkedin.com/in/deekhanduja

Instagram

@deekhanduja

Career Queenz

https://www.facebook.com/careerqueenz

Wildly Ambitious Mama Entrepreneurs

https://www.facebook.com/groups/210559246752140

THE SILENCE OF ABUSE

By Karen Saunders

Changes are urgently needed to stamp out the rampant reported and unreported domestic violence incidents that are increasing annually.

If you're wondering why I'm so passionate about this subject, it's because I have been a victim of domestic violence in all three of my past relationships. That immediately raises the question of how did I allow that to happen? I think I've worked it out – these are my thoughts.

Even though the sun was shining that day as I walked to primary school, I had an overwhelming sense of gloom and a 'knowing' that my life was going to feel akin to climbing a never-ending steep mountain. Since my parents' separation the prior year, I had been looking after myself. Up until this day, I had been coping. Suddenly, life took on another perspective for me, even though I was only 10-years-old.

My parents had recently divorced, their relationship was toxic, both had terrible tempers, and there was violence and domestic abuse. It's only since writing this that I realize not only was my mother abused but so was I. I remember on my 8th birthday, my mother was sleeping in the spare bed in my room. My father came into my room in the morning and tipped my mother off the bed onto the floor. He was yelling and screaming that my sister and I were not to leave my bedroom. We sat there all day, only being allowed to sit on the back step for a brief time during the day. I also recalled   after their divorce, when I was still 10-years-old, going to stay with my Dad for the weekend. I'm assuming it was one of the access weekends. I remember feeling very scared as my father lay on top of me on the couch. Something didn't feel right to me, and the next minute, he got very angry with me and ordered me to bed. He promptly left the house. Looking back, I am sure I dodged a bullet that day, as years later, I discovered he had been sexually abusing my sister for many years.

I can recall tempers raging, Mum being in bed with bruises, cuts, and a burst eardrum. Dad tipping my mother out of bed and onto the floor, things being thrown around the room, and smashed plates of food. Those are my early recollections. My father remarried almost immediately, and my mother remarried when I was 14. Those second marriages also failed. Both stepparents had issues with alcohol dependence.

By that stage, I was emotionally damaged. Absent and abusive parents, abusive stepparents, and no extended family to speak of meant I spent lots of time alone. By the time I was approaching fifteen-years-old, I had left school to work as an apprentice hairdresser. I knew the time was coming with my mother and stepfather when I would have to get out and support myself. I was working long hours and rarely home, but my stepfather wanted me out of the house.

Just before turning seventeen, his ultimatum came. My mother must choose between him or me. I thanked the heavens I had been able to put myself into a position of being able to support myself. I looked at my mother and said, "It's okay, Mum, I will go." At that stage, I was a third-year apprentice, earning $60 per week and paying $32 per week for a furnished flat. As tough as that sounds, the positive side is, I learned how to budget, a very useful skill!

Something is off in our society. By off, I mean toxic and calling for our immediate attention. It is a global issue in society, not just within Australia. It has the propensity to become intergenerational, as it has with me. No woman deserves to live in fear for her or her children's emotional or physical safety and well-being.

I met my husband-to-be when I was twenty-two. I didn't believe in love, as such, and was young, insecure, and desperate to create the family I'd never had, along with the picket fence dream. Although this relationship lasted for 14 years, it was not a happy one. I persevered as I was determined our children would not go through the un-happy experience of a broken home as I had.

At the time, I didn't understand that walking on eggshells around my husband and trying to find the best time to say something so as not to start a tirade from him was actually a consequence of his emotional abuse. To me, it felt nor-mal and what I'd witnessed daily since being a young child.

Any request that we try to work on our relationship ended in me crying after his angry outbursts, blaming me be-cause of my messed-up family upbringing. For example, if I was late after collecting the children from kindergarten or school, I would not be spoken to for up to two weeks. After some time, I was beginning to find it difficult to even get out of bed in the mornings. Fortunately, a friend could see me struggling and suggested I see a psychiatrist she knew of.

My weekly visits lasted for a year before I left him, and for almost a year afterward. I can say, with hand-on-heart, that doctor saved my life. She helped me to see hope, be-lieve in myself, restored my confidence, and assisted in ways to help me find solutions for myself.

Over time, I began to see a way out of the 'black hole' I felt I was in. I had always worked while the children were young, working several part-time jobs. By this stage, my husband was not working, and our financial state was dire.

I began full-time study in Office Administration to allow myself future job prospects and continued working two part-time jobs while studying. It was during this year of study when things became worse.

By this time, there was no help with the children from my husband. I would set out each morning, often with three different drop-off points for the children, prior to attending TAFE. After school, starting the various pick-ups before getting home and doing all the required duties, cooking, baths, and bedtime routines, etc., I was living as a single parent despite being married.

After learning from my eldest son that his father had caused the bruises I questioned him about on his back, I ramped up my search for somewhere to move. Eventually, I found a rental property not too far away to maintain a level of consistency for the children. As I look back, it is plain to see there was domestic abuse in the form of emotional abuse. Emotional abuse is just as serious as physical abuse. It undermines one's confidence and puts doubt into your mind, which can create a whole range of other issues. As an example, my husband taunted me about my study, telling me I would never make it in the corporate world, and who would ever employ me anyway?

In my case, the abuse continued after the marriage ended, via the children. I can see there were definite periods of depression in my life. However, I was fortunate to have the strength of character and resilience to use many of the tools the psychiatrist had taught me during our sessions. The bottom line is if you are a victim of any kind of domestic abuse – get help!

During these years, I continued caring for the children on my own and wore many hats. There was no financial support from their father. Three years after separation, we settled financially with a 50/50 split, and, with $30,000, I was able to borrow and buy a home. Fast forward almost nine years, and after thousands of hours spent laboring on the renovation, I sold the home, making what I thought at the time was an incredible profit, and purchased a larger home within the same area. Again, I spent weekends being Mum's taxi, sports coach, and renovator and sold a year later for a tidy profit. My aim was to ensure security for myself and, ultimately, give my children a head start in life, financially.

After completing my studies, I secured a full-time job, and, eventually, I was fortunate enough to be able to take advantage of an opportunity within this role. I began studying engineering part-time and completed my diploma, leaving a few extra modules completed toward a degree. I also cared for my mother, who was often in the hospital for months at a time. I'm sure most mothers look back when their children have grown and ponder on the 'what ifs' associated with raising them. I know I was not the perfect mother as I was stretched so thin, but I can honestly say I did the very best I could and always with the best intentions.

The statistics are not just scary but horrifying. Our systems are failing us. We must:

- make the necessary changes required across the Family and Magistrate courts for speedier and less costly resolutions;
- provide police education to ensure our frontline battle in the domestic violence world is fully educated and has zero tolerance for officers who do not take the issues and signals seriously enough;
- review the penalties for perpetrators, with harsher consequences for these acts of violence, and; ensure these statistics decline, instead of continuing to soar in the future.

We hear or read about only a fraction of the cases of domestic violence in the media. There are frightening published statistics available online; however, we should also be aware of the cases which are not reported, and therefore are unacknowledged in the ever-growing victim count.

According to MamaMia online news, within a recent eighteen-day period, eight women in Australia died from domestic violence. COVID-19, and the subsequent lockdowns, have raised the daily reporting of domestic abuse. According to an article in The Age Newspaper in June 2020, the United Nations Population Fund has predicted that for every three months the lockdowns continue, an additional 15 million cases of domestic violence will occur worldwide.

In Australia, I doubt there were many people who did not feel pain and deep sorrow about the terribly heart-breaking incident reported recently in the news. Hannah Clarke and her three children were torched to death in a car by her ex-partner. This man had recently violated a Family Violence Order. He was due to face court, but in the interim, he was left free from penalty. He was able to get to his victims (his family) before he was made to answer to the law.

My immediate reaction was, "Why was he allowed to be free in society if he had breached the court orders?" The intervention order had been granted because there was a clear and present danger to the woman and her family. Yet there were no immediate repercussions for a breach. How many women across the globe are potentially in the same boat as this family right now?

In 2016, Clare Blumer from ABC News reported Australian police are dealing with 5,000 domestic and family violence matters a week. That's one every two minutes, or 264,028 per year, which was an increase of 7% in 2015.

And how many extended family members are also victims who suffer the peripheral consequences of family violence? According to Victorian government crime statistics, 58,164 people fell into this category in our state alone over the five year period to 2019. Imagine the impact globally!

By this stage, I was in another relationship, but we didn't live together. I was protective of my children and was not willing to put them through any stepparent situations due to my own history. The children were not involved with him, aside from the rare café catch-up. I would go out with him on a Saturday night when the children were with their father, or I could collect my mother to stay at home with them.

Although initially there were definite positives for me in this relationship, it also became abusive. Unfortunately, this time it was both emotional and physical abuse.

At that time, domestic or family violence was not taken as seriously in our society. One night, when the children were with their father, and I had been out for the evening with my abuser, he became violent. I was beaten with the metal rod from my vacuum cleaner, hair ripped out by being dragged around by it, and I was bruised and battered. Items had been smashed and thrown by him. I was finally able to call the police to attend my house after I had been held hostage inside my own home for over three hours. The police attended while he was still there and told me that if I wanted to take an Intervention Order out against him, I should go to the police station the next day.

I stayed with friends for a few nights and then attended the Magistrates Court to obtain an Interim Intervention Order. I also attended the police station to make a formal complaint and asked for assault charges to be laid. They photographed the extensive bruising, I made my official statement and expected justice to be served. However, that was not to be.

The senior officer at the station called me in to see him, whereby he explained to me the police would not be pressing charges against him as I was not in the hospital, nothing was broken, and I wasn't dead.

At the final hearing for the Domestic Violence Intervention order, I was awarded an Intervention Order, which was enduring, not the usual 2-year period.

After coming out of that relationship shattered, having been through so much with the thought pattern of, "I can help this person who is struggling with mental issues if ONLY I can get through to him and make him see how happy we could be; if only he would get help." I was not able to share the problems for fear my friends would think less of him, just in case we could get past the problems.

I believe that's a common mistake most women make. Firstly, you cannot rescue people from their demons, and secondly, the REAL issue was that I didn't value myself enough to end it before it became so ugly.

How are we allowing this to happen in our society? What occurred in these men's lives to think it's acceptable to be physically, sexually, emotionally, financially, or psychologically abusive? That the threatening, coercive behaviour which controls or dominates a woman, or anyone, for that matter, is justified? How do these perpetrators make women feel that their actions are her fault for making them angry? Or justify their behaviour by saying they were just letting off steam? Or that they had been wronged? Where is the ownership of their abusive behavior?

Our system and the apathy in society require an extensive overhaul. We must help men to recognize their own issues before they turn into another domestic violence statistic. We need, as part of the curriculum in schools, to include more education around mental health to assist in reducing the stigma associated. This may change the mindset of people, so they seek the same help with a mental health issue as they would for a broken bone. This has improved greatly over the ensuing years; however, there is still much work to be done.

We need to stand up and call it out when we witness abuse. We also need to get these abusers off the street so they don't have the opportunity to commit these horrible crimes. Over recent times, similar crimes were committed by Rowen Baxter, Boris Ristevski, Greg Anderson, Robert Farquharson, Gerard Baden-Clay, Haoling Luo, and Arthur Freeman, to name but a few.

Governments must stop wasting money on inept services, spend what is allocated more effectively, and invest more resources to eliminate this scourge from society. Changes are required in both the social and justice systems.

Five years passed, and the children were grown and getting on with their lives. My career was ticking along nicely, and finally, I was in reasonable shape financially, after working hard and renovating and selling two properties. I had met other men over the years, but nobody I felt was quite right for me. I was confident in my own self-worth, and my life was on track. I didn't believe I needed to settle for less than my worth – it had to be the right fit.

I was comfortable with the thought of being single for the rest of my life when, out of the blue, I met what I thought was the man of my dreams. He seemed fun and appeared to share similar belief patterns and values to my own. We fell in love quickly, and I rented my property out and moved in with him within a couple of months. We purchased an investment property based on my income and equity in my home. Life was great for the first two years, and I thanked my lucky stars every day.

Then the cracks began to show. Because of the fabulous two years, I swept away any concerns I had. I told myself he was having a rough patch or excused his unsettling behaviours in other ways. In hindsight, it's easy to see that the abuse started in small, insidious ways. Over the next several years, the 'bad' times became more frequent, but again, I put it down to financial stress or found other excuses for him, preferring to forgive and forget.

Seven years later, after using my superannuation to get us into a house in Queensland and get through some challenging times business-wise, we moved back to Melbourne to renovate the property I owned before meeting him. After the renovation, I sold it for a great profit. We had fallen in love with the idea of living on acreage just outside of Melbourne. We found the perfect spot and were mortgage-free in our home. My dream!

It was during that final year on the property that things became unbearable, and I could no longer make excuses for his behaviour. It seems this is often the case when an abuser gets you away from your support networks. There weren't any neighbors to hear his frequent irrational and abusive outbursts, usually lasting for three days and nights. We were renovating the property and living off the proceeds of the sale of my home. I was teary and depressed and sought help from my GP. She recognized the gaslighting I was experiencing and immediately put me on a mental health plan. The psychologist I saw suggested I speak with a local organization for Family Violence, as he felt I needed safety tactics and plans should matters at home get out of hand. After the situation escalated into angry, physical threats, I called a friend who suggested I gather some basics and get the hell out of there. I thought that would be the end of the abuse!

More has to be done to change attitudes. In my case, when the police officer who told me that this man was just letting off steam when he had me cornered and seething in my face just how much of a 'slapping' I deserved and how much he wanted to do it. Or, perhaps, 17 years earlier, the attitude of the senior police officer who told me they wouldn't be pressing charges on my ex after the physical abuse I received which left me black and blue because I wasn't in the hospital, nothing was broken, and I wasn't dead – there is no longer room for these attitudes.

Sadly, it was just the beginning of different kinds of abuse via texts, phone calls, and emails. Despite obtaining a Family Violence Intervention Order, financial abuse continues in a very different format. As I had always been the person to manage finances, including all properties, I continued doing so after I left the relationship with no contribution from him; my aim is to ensure there were no foreclosures on property mortgages, as this would cause damage to the financial future for both of us. On the other hand, he has done his utmost within the legal system to ensure I have no access to funds.

The repercussions of that have seen me virtually couch surfing with friends and family for months on end, while the offender sits quite happily in the mortgage-free property that was purchased from the sale of my home. The system does not protect you from this, and unfortunately, with the current COVID-19 pandemic, the already overburdened and under-performing Family Court system has been woefully affected. The Magistrates Court system for the Family Violence Order has also been affected by the lockdowns, with hearing dates being blown out by months. It could take years for this to be resolved in the court system.

Life throws curve balls for sure, for some more often than others. But, whatever the case, we all have challenges throughout our journeys. I wouldn't be in this position if I received correct legal advice before purchasing properties. Instead of buying the properties in joint names, to protect my assets, the properties should have been made tenants in common with a percentage of ownership for each party. Even though there have been many tough days, and no doubt many more to come, I thank my lucky stars for my resilience, my wonderful family and friends, and the knowledge that one day this will be over, and I will once again be in control of what happens next.

During my journey, I have discovered I am a strong and resilient person who is worthy of being treated with respect and love. I have learned how to deal with symptoms of anxiety, and I endeavor to make a point of finding gratitude for something every day. I have learned to 'live in the now' and let go of worry regarding my future. I choose to concern myself with only the things I can change and disregard anything out of my control.

For any victim who is currently suffering from domestic abuse, my hope is to encourage you to seek the assistance you need to make a change knowing you ARE worth more, that you DESERVE better, you CAN start a new life. No matter what, we cannot change the past, but with higher self-worth and self-love, you can change your future.

The bottom line for me is this. To protect yourself from being included as a victim of the ever-increasing family violence numbers, NEVER avoid or ignore the warning signs. Never give the benefit of the doubt repeatedly. Value yourself. Believe in your worth and learn and understand how to protect yourself financially.

About Karen Saunders

Karen Saunders lives in Melbourne Australia and has had a varied career. Most recently she has been working in insolvency, assisting people or organisations to resolve debt issues. She has studied NLP and hypnotherapy and is working towards utilising these skills, along with her life experience, to transition into an author and therapist/life coach. Her passion lies in aiding survivors of Domestic Abuse. Writing has been on her bucket list and her goal is to focus on personal growth and self-help books.

Karen Babinall (Saunders)

LinkedIn - https://www.linkedin.com/in/karen-babinall-bb32b8198/

Facebook -https://www.facebook.com/karen.saunders.12382923/

FREEDOM WITHIN

By Ian Maxwell

Job security and the days of employees and employers being loyal and supporting each other through good and bad times have long vanished. Today's corporate behavior prefers profitability over all other aspects of a business. It has no morals or emotions about cutting headcount, even just before Christmas (ho, ho, ho), to meet financial objectives in the future. Regrettably, the experience of being cut from your job, made redundant, retrenched, or otherwise laid off, can have a profound and personal effect on your life in multiple ways, ranging from practical financial concerns to the mental impact on your self-confidence and feelings of self-worth.

This is a story of how I navigated through two separate redundancies, one divorce, one country relocation, and the bereavement of both parents. How I managed myself, recovered, and evolved into a happier and more balanced individual, although my current wife might argue with me about my use of the word "balanced."

If you are presently experiencing or working through a tough period, I hope my story can inspire you to look for the light at the end of the tunnel. My purpose in writing is to share my experience, observations, and learning, and hopefully encourage others to move forward with positivity. I want to help you find a new skip in your step in a similar way as I have done.

My Story

I have devoted my entire career to the automotive industry and have experienced many roles and functions in both retail and engineering. I lost my first position in September 2012 at the age of 47. I was also just a few months after my first marriage had officially failed. Both are major life events, significant enough on their own. Each is also life-changing, but sadly my experience is not unique, and I wouldn't wish anyone to go through either of them, especially so close together. The cumulative effect was quite difficult to deal with; these events kind of magnified my emotions at the time, which took a bit of dealing with.

The job loss was due to a change in company ownership and a reorganization. The company I was running shut down due to a change in the business strategy, which was never fully explained to the people it affected. The off-handed way the parent company handled it affected me badly and left me feeling very angry. My location in Malaysia complicated my life even further. As a British National working in Kuala Lumpur, finding another job was a big problem for me. I could always move back to the UK, but after 12 years working in Kuala Lumpur, my life, networking avenues, and contacts were in Asia. Rather than relocate back to the UK, I decided to seek new work in Asia.

After 18 months of anguish and soul searching, I was excited and very happy to land a new job based in Singapore. I had already moved down to the city-state and started work early in 2014. Life was going well, and I had settled nicely when I married again in 2015, but the calm didn't last. It was with a horrible sense of déjà vu by the end of 2018. As Christmas was around the corner, I became the victim of another corporate decision and lost my job. I guess it's never easy for anyone to give bad news, but some attempt at empathy from your boss would go some way to ease the impact. That didn't happen, and the effect on me was again, devastating. For a second time, I found myself unemployed and wondering what to do next, except this time, it was slightly different. I was now over 50-years-old and the disappointing phrase "overqualified" would come up more and more often as I searched for a new job.

As I searched, 2019 was not a good year. I was already anxious about the future, then my father passed away in March, and then my mother in April. They had both been ill for some time, and while none of it was a surprise, it was still a shock. I spent a good deal of time travelling between Singapore and the UK, where my parents and the wider family lived, but shortly after my mother's funeral, my out-look on life took a step change. It was one of those turning points or light bulb moments, except this one didn't sud-denly light up, but instead moved from a faint glow into a fully lit bulb over a couple of months.

Somehow, fantastically, I became set free, not from any sort of responsibility or repression from my parents or family, but from my own thoughts and a fear of how others viewed me. I hadn't realized it, but I had been fixated on things I could not change, and at the same time subcon-sciously worried about what others were thinking about me. All my job searching had been for positions attuned to my self-perceived status and how I would appear to my peers. Now, I realized the only person who needed to like what I was doing was me (and perhaps my wife). This was the start of my transition to more independent thinking and a happier   life. The change allowed me to stop worrying and start planning. I began working at the things I could control, not the things I could not control. If you read on, I will try to explain what I learned.

Think of Job Loss as a Journey

We can usually sense when something is wrong at work, and from the moment you know your job is at risk and you are   retrenched, you are committed to a journey. You didn't choose to take this route, but one you will have to complete regardless of how you feel about it. Sometimes it's merely a mental journey as your mind adjusts to a new normal, and sometimes it's both a mental and physical journey as you end up living someplace new.

Whatever happens, you will be highly likely to spend a lot of time thinking about things you cannot control. We all do this. It's human behavior and a feature that apparently sets us apart from the animals. We can imagine what life will be like if this or that happens. Humans can visualize a future and regret the past, whereas your pet dog, for example, cannot imagine what life would be like if he had two tails or a new ball to chase. It is our burden as humans that our minds can come up with all sorts of imaginary scenarios and issues and cause self-inflicted worry and stress. Self-torment is one way to describe it, and it will start as soon as you sense something is not safe with your job. The extent to which you are then emotionally affected by the job loss depends a lot on the way you are released by your employer, who, by the way, might not be skilled in delivering bad news and might not consider the impact they have on the person.

Several major life events can place us under extreme emotional stress. Some of these events are a divorce, the death of someone close, moving to a new home, changing schools or jobs, a physical accident, or an illness. All are examples of significant events that can take us on an uninvited emotional journey. The only certainty is that when something life-changing happens, you will be wrestling with your thoughts and imagination a lot of the time.

It is my experience that the loss of a job has a similar range of emotions to those that I have experienced with a bereavement. In 1969, the American Swiss Psychiatrist, Elisabeth Kübler-Ross, proposed there were five stages of grief. *"Denial, anger, bargaining, depression, and acceptance."* I can certainly say that when I experienced the job loss, the dominant emotion for me was anger. I clearly remember being angry at my former employer and bosses, and quite significantly, myself for somehow "allowing" it to happen, like I could have done something to avoid it. Depression came later and was a stage that confused me greatly, but merely being aware of this emotional journey and your own mental hijacking is useful toward understanding yourself, forgiving yourself, and your search for stability. If you are feeling angry or depressed, take a step back and think about the bigger picture. You may be stuck in one of the stages described by Kübler-Ross.

Over time, the Kübler-Ross theory has attracted some critical debate. Still, the idea that I want to suggest is that following a major event such as a job loss, we have to process our emotions, and they will move through stages that change over time. In reality, this is not a one-time journey through the emotions, and we will often re-live the events in our minds and experience those emotions multiple times. I call this a negative thought loop. We may even get stuck in one of the stages and repeatedly visit a specific event and emotion. Sometimes different things will trigger negative thought loops.

Self-Awareness & Negative Thought Loops

When we become unemployed, we get to have lots of time to ourselves. It's the eternal trade-off. If you have the time, you don't have the money, and if you have the money, you rarely have the time. Time for your mind to reflect and think, which might sound nice, but I assure you, can be no fun at all when unemployed. Each time I lost my job, I found my thoughts would easily drift into negative thought loops, re-living the worst experiences, and playing on the self-doubt that lives in the dark corners of the mind. Often, this happened when I was doing routine household tasks such as washing up. What could I have done differently? Was it my fault? What did I do wrong? Why me?

These thought loops of self-blame are destructive. Your confidence and self-belief are undermined, and you are left feeling pretty miserable. The situation is further compounded because subconsciously, we tend to associate the negative thought loops with whatever household task we were doing when we first had them. It took some time to identify this was happening to me, and then a bit longer to work out how to change the situation.

Experiencing the same negative thought loop each time we do something mundane such as the washing up, is a total pain in the neck. For a while, I disliked showering, which is not the best thing when your self-confidence is low, and you need people to like you. I cannot explain why, but every time I stepped into my shower, I would think about one specific negative situation, and the emotional journey would start again. I would come out of the shower feeling exhausted and anxious instead of clean and refreshed.

It is a massive step forward when we become self-aware enough to identify the moments when you head off down the rabbit hole of your own thoughts, regrets, and fears. Recognizing when you are setting off on a negative thought loop and interrupting that thought pattern is genuinely liberating. It also means you can go back to washing up and stop avoiding the shower, which also makes everyone around you happy.

But how do we interrupt the thought loop? First, you have to recognize you're doing it. Then you have to stop the thought train. Interrupt it and consciously choose to shift your thinking to something you can control, such as what to eat for dinner or what color to paint the kitchen. Essentially, I think about anything positive and avoid anything I cannot control, such as the past.

Sometimes, before you can change and interrupt a specific thought loop, you need to acknowledge the negative thoughts and allow them to conclude. Compare this in much the same way as when you get a song stuck in your head. Sing the song in your head until it ends, and you get closure and an opportunity to move onto a new song. Being aware of when to allow this will let you accelerate your thoughts quickly to a conclusion, and then you are free to adopt a new thought about something you can control.

Open Yourself Up

One other area I have worked hard on, which has made a big difference to my happiness has been the decision to be more open. If you have ever watched the 2008 movie "Yes Man" starring Jim Carrey, you will have seen an entertaining idea of the effect saying yes to everything can have. In the film, the main character is magically bound to say yes to any request, which makes for an interesting comedy. It's an extreme example, but using the spirit of that movie, at the midpoint of 2019, I made a promise to myself that I would open myself to as many opportunities as I possibly could. If someone invited me to attend a free seminar, I said yes. If someone suggested we meet for a catchup coffee, I said yes.

The effect this decision had on my life has been extraordinary. I don't tend to think of myself as a highly social person. In fact, I chose to work in engineering because mechanical things don't tend to talk back, at least not yet. I am quite happy working alone, and previously I would have avoided complicated social situations such as networking events, especially ones where I knew nobody.

As a result of consciously pushing myself to be open to new people and new things, I have attended numerous self-development trainings, online trainings, seminars, and even Chef school. I have evolved past the self-limiting restrictions I didn't know I had placed on myself, expanded my experiences, and spent time with a wide range of interesting people who cumulatively have helped restore some of my faith in mankind.

New friendships have led to other new people, and I am slowly transitioning into a new world of entrepreneurship. I regularly brainstorm ideas with people who are equally interested in being positive, and, yes, it's challenging. Still, it's also fun, and at the age of 55, I am learning new skills relevant to the 4th industrial revolution and Industry 4.0.

I have launched myself as a private chef in Singapore and started a business as a private Chef with a "Home Dining" concept while building an online platform for bringing basic cooking skills to people through video conferencing and a web portal.

As I write this in August 2020, I have now been out of the corporate world for 21 months. Some of that time has been very difficult, but I am very thankful for the love and support from my wife, who has encouraged me to evolve and reshape my own thinking. I hope there is someone in your life who can do the same, but if there isn't, my advice is to be kind to yourself, set your goals, and work to participate in the new economy.

Now, more than ever, I realize life is an ongoing work in progress with no such thing as happily ever after, but we can deal with the curve balls by being self-aware and open. Doing this has helped me find positivity and enjoyment while continually re-inventing and upgrading myself.

If you have invested your time to read this story, be assured you are already taking a positive approach to improving your life. I believe in you and wish you success and happiness.

About Ian Maxwell

Originally from Norfolk in the UK, Ian has lived in Asia since 2001. Following a successful 30 plus years working in the automotive industry with iconic brands such as Lotus, Bentley & Volvo Ian has now turned his attention towards helping others transition from the corporate office to their own plan B's.

Ian remains based in Singapore where he is now indulging his passion as a private chef, offering home dining experiences and private cookery classes. Ian also recently embarked on delivering a weight management and wellness program and now considers himself to be an emerging Entrepreneur.

Married to a Singaporean wife, Ian and his wife have four grown up children, one grandchild (so far), two dogs and a lot of home improvement projects to complete.

LinkedIn: www.linkedin.com/in/ian-maxwell

Facebook : https://www.facebook.com/MaxWellnesssg-105509271215215

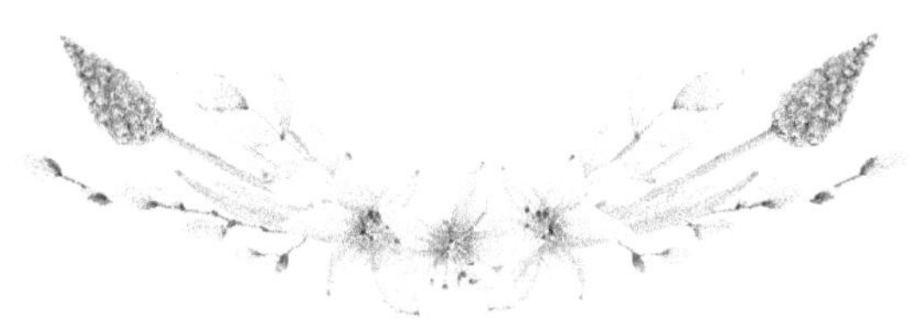

STEP UP & RISE TO A NEW WORLD ORDER.

By Nishith Bhatnagar

While glancing through my photos for a specific snapshot of a family event at the end of Dec.2019, I found myself wondering how many of us could see the pandemic gripping the globe in a matter of a couple of months, bringing the global economy to a standstill, and a majority of humankind under forced lockdown?

Did we??? Did anyone??? Of course not!!!!

These times are unlike anything experienced in our lifetime.

Not even one person could foresee this pandemic producing the devastating loss of human lives and still have no cure nor end date in sight. We were swarmed with a seemingly endless train of contradictory posts in print, as well as electronic media, each claiming with more conviction the message being propagated. One became increasingly confused about what to expect in the days to come and how to respond to this emergent crisis faced by humankind.

This **"Great Lockdown"** will be the worst recession since the **"Great Depression"** of the 1930s. Already, many current economic matrices are matching to those records set almost a hundred years back. There is considerable uncertainty about what the economy will look like when we emerge from this lockdown.

But then ...! Even in tragic times, stress and grief of any magnitude must be practically overcome somewhere down the line!

No matter what we go through, it is   Hope & Hope alone of a brighter future that leads us to persist and to persevere.

So, the good news is! Ultimately, like all other earlier crises, this one too shall pass!

The Virus is going to stay, and we humans will have to learn to live with the problem for at least a few more years! We, as humans, are incredibly resilient & adaptable! Eventually, we will find a way!

The scars of the economic meltdown will be the next major challenge to overcome, especially with the projected downtrends for the next few years: the all-time high unemployment rate and the imminent re-alignment in the global socio-political order, to name a few.

In these **unprecedented times,** how do we, as Leaders, Entrepreneurs, and Independent Business Owners respond?

Amidst all this, we must act with exceptional Ingenuity to navigate oneself away from uncertainty toward purposefulness and conviction. Only those of *us* who choose to respond proactively and who have a strategic plan in place will be the forerunners in the new world order!

So … Do we have any plan in place???

I see too many people saying out loud:

"How can anyone plan when there is so much uncertainty?"

"No plan can succeed under such circumstances!"

Today, beyond all doubt, there is so much uncertainty regarding everything; Industrial, Social, Cultural, and Environmental conditions, business models, and other such scenarios that may emerge after the lifting of the lockdown.

However, it is also true that this extreme uncertainty also creates unique opportunities for personal growth for individuals and exponential growth for businesses.

There is a learning opportunity in every crisis; however difficult or painful a situation it may be. Some of the most profound realizations come under challenging conditions. When we are confronted with the reality of who we are and how we live, it broadens the horizon for how life can be and what is most important. We realize what we can indeed be, and how much we can persevere under such trying times.

Just quick research on the internet will prove that after most of the major crises faced by humankind in the past few hundred years, significant accomplishments, inventions, explorations, and businesses have emerged and flourished while the majority of traditional practices were relegated to history.

The point is those scientists, scholars, businessmen, and industries did find opportunities to grow during those tumultuous times. So, talking in terms of history, the present crisis is not entirely unprecedented, with context to test the infinite capacity of the human spirit to persist and persevere under extreme situations.

To realize one's potential to its maximum, one needs first to clear their ***"why"*** and then ***"what"*** and ***"how"*** will follow, as explained by Simon Sinek in his famous Golden Circle's Theory.

To clear the ***"why,"*** the associated objectives, passions, emotions, and the value to the actual act need to be firmed. With the purpose of being defined up to a non-negotiable state, then further what actions are required to be taken and methods to be followed can be effectively worked out.

Having to face the uncertainties, we have an alternate perspective:

"Uncertainty can be put to our advantage if strategically addressed."

Executing this as a strategy, unique disruptive ideas, and value propositions are to be effectively implemented to target the hidden opportunities in an environment, generally considered a potential risk by the market, thus positioning yourself differentially against your competitors.

Traditionally, the different types of business risks are seen as something to be mitigated and managed for the potential consequences of the potential risks. What this means is with the focus being on known risks; firstly, the unknown risks do not get covered, they can strike at any time, and secondly, the opportunities get lost due to heavy protectionism against perceived risk scenarios.

For putting uncertainties to one's advantage, the out-of-the-box thought process is utilized to target the hidden opportunities. In this case, a strategy is devised to perceive the unknown as a uniquely differentiating value proposition for the self, thus leading to a chance to execute bold and innovative solutions, effectively positioning oneself to an advantage.

I have found that *Utilizing the First Principles* concepts, the ambiguities and uncertainties of these times can mainly be addressed to develop suitable strategic plans for our respective businesses.

Research tells us that reasoning by *first principles* is most useful when you are either doing something for the very first time or dealing with a situation involving a high degree of complexity or understanding a situation that you're having problems with.

There are a few key points here. First, problem statements must be framed correctly through asking the right questions, and second, is to challenge the status quo, i.e., to identify and question the relevance of the assumptions concerning the changing environment.

Reasoning by *first principles* frees the essentials from the shroud of assumptions and conventions. Typically, we hear: **"This is how things get done here"** or **"We tried this earlier, and it did not work."** Another one commonly said is: **"This proposal will   never be acceptable"** and **"Because I am telling you so."** Mostly these generic statements will be assumed to be correct or conclusive and will be limiting in nature. Once the essentials are evident in free form, innovative solutions to real issues can be found.

The real power of *first principles* thinking is moving away from incremental improvement and into possibility. When we limit ourselves to improving a given situation.

Within the realm of the existing environment, it will always be incremental thinking as there will always be a limit to which a current process or an activity can be improved without changing its totality.

It is when we step back and reflect on what is possible while focusing on the essentials that we see what is possible. Its then, and only then, real solutions emerge to achieve the concentrated objectives beyond the existing process or environment or other limiting conditions.

The first principles are established through a detailed analysis process to develop the essential while questioning the assumptions systematically. This involves clearing the purpose, challenging the status quo, exploring for evidence and alternatives, and finally drawing a conclusion along with the impact and implications of the findings. Decisions arrived at by following this process are found to be more effective in the long run.

As a key take away, there are three factors critical to creating a strategic plan to meet the challenges of the new world order effectively. These are namely the three R's.

 # Reflect, # Re-orient, and # Re-Claim.

#1: To Reflect: This is to pause & step back a little and have a high-level perspective of the overall situation where we find ourselves now.

- ❖ To get our Purpose Clear and the Problem statement defined correctly.
- ❖ List the essentials and the revised objectives.

- ❖ Analyse the situation concerning the changed environment or other conditions.
- ❖ Explore hidden opportunities and the risks related to present uncertainties.
- ❖ Explore alternatives and analyse their Impacts and Aspects.
- ❖ Find a single disruptive idea or differentiating value proposition for yourself.

#2: To ReOrient: This is to adapt to the changing business environment, deal with reality, and seize opportunities that others cannot see. Digitization is in, in a big way. Traditional business models are on the way out. Being Inline is fast changing to being Online. One-to-one is out, and One-to-many is in.

- ❖ Reorient yourself and your business to align with your one disruptive idea or Differentiating Value proposition. Reframe your Policies and Procedures and to reposition your brand as per the demands of your strategic plan.
- ❖ Inspire Innovation in self and the team, create a conducive environment to encourage asymmetrical thinking and or Out-of-the-Box solutions to manage new challenges and target hidden opportunities of the new world order.
- ❖ Reorientation involves setting up a new work culture devoid of assumptions and biases. Fast adaptability and response to market demands will be the key to survival.

❖ The adoption of automation, digital, and other new technologies should be used to your advantage.

 # 3. To Reclaim: This is to go all out for your Dreams, Goals, and Passions with whatever it takes to achieve and Reclaim what each one of us is genuinely capable of becoming, Your Best Version!

❖ Have your "Why" clear. Have the Big Picture always in perspective!
❖ Not Achieving is not an option!
❖ Having belief in oneself is key to maximizing one's potential.
❖ Have your daily affirmations in place.
❖ Get Quality Feedback from your mentor frequently to keep on track.

I genuinely believe the best time of our lives is just lurking around the corner, waiting to be reclaimed by every one of us!

We are the Seekers.

We are the Believers.

So, **Step up and Rise to a New World Order**.

About Nishith Prakash Bhatnagar

He is an Entrepreneur, Keynote Speaker, Transformation Coach & Mentor.A Mechanical engineer by Profession, Automobile Professional by choice & specializing as a change agent in the field of Business Excellence & amp; Lean Thinking!

Having had the opportunity to get associated with multiple corporates, he has a rich exposure of developing the right mindset, work environment & the thought process essential for creation of the strategic plans for turning around any business.

Nishith is happily married with Preeti, an enthusiast in social works and have one son, who is an Engineer and a daughter, who is a Fashion Designer.

He can be contacted at:

Mail: np.bhatnagar@gmail.com ,

Linked in: https://www.linkedin.com/in/nishith-prakash-bhatnagar-3636609

Facebook: https://www.facebook.com/nishith.bhatnagar.1

Instagram: Instagram.com/npb.newone/

Twitter: @NP_Bhatnagar

FALL TO LEARN

By Vinson Chua

April 2019

"Hey pa, you're sleeping right now, and when you read this message, I'll be the one sleeping😝 Anyway, I just wanted to tell you this:

I know you're stressed and worried about your work, and it's okay to feel like that. It's okay to let out your emotions; in fact, it's healthy to do so☺ Always know that I believe in you and believe that you'll be able to overcome whatever problems you face in life💜 But, at the same time, you shouldn't be running away from your problems. Ask for help if you need help, you always have my support🐮🐨 You can do it🐈😺 Love you always😍🐱"

This was a WhatsApp message from my15-years-old daughter while I was in rehabilitation for "depression" the last two months, spending one night at the "Institute of Mental Health," five days at a hospital, and three weeks recuperating at home. It was the most challenging time of my life as a father, husband, and son.

Have you ever felt so small in your life, and success seemed to be so close yet so far away?

This is my journey in chasing that "success" in life, and I hope it can inspire you.

Before this, I was a co-founder of a technology start-up, dreaming of building the next unicorn in the industry, disrupting the industry, and becoming rich!

This dream started with my experience working with Silicon Valley companies back in the 90s. In 2000, I joined a semiconductor start-up and began this journey. When September 11 happened, I was laid off in November 2001, which ended my first foray. Being young and resilient, I managed to find a job quickly and got an overseas job posting to work in Shanghai, China. By then, my first child was one-year-old, and I managed to bring our family over in the first year. We enjoyed many happy moments during the first year, making new friends, gaining unique experience living in a city that is transforming by the day, enjoying four seasons, which we do not get in Singapore, and many other joyful occasions. When we finally settled down in Shanghai, my wife got an opportunity to work with a multinational company, but the position was to be based back in Singapore. This "happy family life" has to come to a stop, as she and my daughter relocated back to Singapore, while I fulfilled the obligation of my employment contract.

In 2003, there was a SARS breakout and living apart from my loved ones took a toll on me. I decided to terminate my contract and be back in Singapore with my family.

Having no job offer, a friend (TS) approached me to help in one of his businesses when his staff quit.

This started the second phase of my chasing money dream. With some luck and persistence, we managed to secure products to distribute and make some decent money until 2013. I was allowed to be an equity owner in this business. An excellent ten-year run, even though there were some low points like the 2008 Financial Crisis, where we needed to cut some losses by closing down some overseas offices. I was still mentally sound and happy. I still recall telling my wife during that time that, "It is good that our bank account is heading toward zero; the only direction it can go next is upward."

I was really blessed during this period. My second and third child were born during this period, where I spent many wonderful times bonding with my family. I had the privilege of watching and spending quality time with my children, watching them grow, and witnessing many milestones in their growing up years. At the same time, I got to enjoy the holidays with my wife, parents, and in-laws.

To ensure that I enjoyed the fruits of my labour if I made it, I took extra efforts to take care of my physical and mental well-being. I changed my lifestyle, bad eating habits, took up distance running, and Qi Gong.

In the back of my mind, I always encouraged myself that if Wealth, Health, and Relationship are the three most important things to achieve in life, I made sure that I passed with good health and a healthy relationship while wealth has not arrived yet!

However, I was always unhappy with my financial situation; I felt insecure as I was constantly worried about the security and stability of my distribution business, as many of our clients had moved production to China. At the same time, I developed a self-centered attitude and jealously over the growth of people around me, including my partner TS, who had built his wealth through his other businesses and investments.

This is where I began searching for the next source of income and opportunity. This affected my focus in the core business and indirectly affected my relationship with TS, who has been very supportive all these years, even when I tried to divert into other industries and did not succeed.

In 2014, I decided to ask TS to let me take over his share since he is already doing very well financially. This was a great mistake I committed, a no gratitude and self-centered mindset. For two months, it was very stressful for me, as I did not have his financial power and worried that I might not negotiate a good deal. This was the first time I experienced sleepless nights in my life. I was known to be able to sleep anywhere and would go to sleep whenever I faced challenges. Eventually, TS was very gracious to offer a reasonable price to take over my share. Our relationship did not turn that sour, but we stopped meeting each other except for sending greetings on special occasions.

We went from good friends and business partners to "superficial" friends. At that time, I was too busy thinking of what to do next and did not really bother much about this lost friendship.

From 2015 to 2018, I explored new business partnerships, working for people, and eventually co-founded a technology start-up (L) and was responsible for business development.

Being the primary breadwinner, I convinced my wife to sell our house and go live with her parents so that we could have a longer runway in my start-up dream pursuit. We even sold our insurance and prepared to do whatever it takes to reach my end goal. We were also very thankful that we managed to secure funding to keep the company afloat during this period.

To keep the operational cost of the company low, we had a lean team, and each of us had to take up additional roles. As I knew that I am not too proficient and interested in technical work, I got my university classmate, CS, to help out in this area from day one. With CS company's (E-Co) support, we managed to secure a high-profile project with the mutual understanding that we will engage E-Co service accordingly. However, when the project was confirmed in 2018, my company's management decided to hire someone else due to a more reasonable cost. I was tasked with the project management and technical work, a role that I am not comfortable with.

This had also affected my relationship with E-Co's boss, which up to this day, we have not reconciled the damaged friendship.

I did not have much time to think then due to a tight project timeframe. I dove into this role and spent about three months learning many new things I initially felt fulfilling. As we proceeded toward completing the project, I started to feel burned   out, helpless and disintegrated. I had many sleepless nights working on solving technical issues.

Though I have an engineering qualification, never in my 25-year career have I done any technical work. I began to dislike my work and had several discussions with my partner to get someone else to take over this role, but there was no concrete conclusion. I started to get lethargic in life, losing interest in my hobbies, favourite food, and even relationships with my loved ones. When my 10-year-old son asked me to play with him, I was "half-interested," and all I wanted was to end the game early so that I can go to sleep or hide. My two teenage daughters may be independent, but I knew in my heart that they knew what was going on and went through this challenging time silently. Thank God, my wife found a lot of strength in herself to hold the fort down and lead the family.

As the days passed by, those sleepless nights turned into a nightmare where I experienced cold sweats, frequent urination, tension from my head to shoulders, head shaking uncontrollably, moaning, and hearing music in my ears. I started to have hallucinations and delusions where my mind would run wild, thinking of all possible scenarios that I would get into deep trouble and fail in the project. Eventually, I developed suicidal thoughts with the music in my ears, turning into a song that kept encouraging me to end my life. I went to see a doctor and was prescribed sleeping pills and mood stabilisers.

During a management meeting, I mistook my partner's (CH) good intention to take me off the project role and decided to quit. During the handover, I suddenly collapsed and was unable to work at all. Amazingly, my wife stepped in and helped to complete the project with help from my partners. She even took up the challenge to take over some of my duties to keep the company going.

This happened just before the Chinese New Year (CNY) 2019 period and was traumatic for everyone. My mind could not stop thinking, everything that came into my thoughts would be the worst possible outcome from my relationships with my wife, my kids, my relatives, friends, business partners, career, health, and so on. I spent each day fighting between the "evil thoughts" of ending my life or getting back on my feet! I was very thankful that my China-based sister and brother-in-law, who were visiting Singapore at the time, spent a lot of time watching over and counseling me. With their encouragement, I also started attending church, read the bible, and worked on the spiritual side of my life.

On the first day of CNY, I was still unwell and not interested in celebrating or meeting people. I even found reasons to chase away relatives who were visiting my mother, who was living with me. My siblings then made the decision for her to live with my brother to protect her from seeing me in this state. By the third day of CNY, my suicidal thoughts had become worse; **I even started planning how to end my life.** The lack of sleep and toxic thoughts had also caused significant damage to my body and mind. I spoke with my wife, sister, and brother-in-law, that I need professional help.

They decided to check me into the Institute of Mental Health (IMH), the authority in Singapore, for treating mental illness. Patients here belong to the "high risk" group and live in a locked-up environment. I was locked in a hall about the size of two basketball courts with people who were tied to their chairs   ir and shouted   or moaned the whole day; people who smile and greet you regularly; and people who exhibit insane behaviours. It was both shock therapy for me and also a devastating experience. Seeing the worst that I could end up   motivated me to recover as fast as I could. I did not want to end up like some of the inmates who had been there for months. At the same time, I was very concerned with the potential social stigma if my future employers, friends, and relatives found out about my stay in this place. How am I to get back to   everyday life, a regular job, and be the husband, father, and son I should be? These became my new "toxic thoughts."

Again, my wife, the wonder woman in my life, came to the rescue. She found another more suitable hospital for me and sent me there the next day. I spent almost a week there working on my rehab and self-reflection.

At the hospital, I felt very guilty for letting my children down, as I promised them, "Children, medical cost bills in Singapore are very expensive. The best gift that I could give them was to stay healthy so that I would not be a burden to the family." Here I am, reflecting in the hospital about what has happened to my years of healthy living, working on both the body and mind. I also felt very embarrassed that my wife was now the "head" of the family, making all the decisions, and supporting the family. I began to work on the fastest recovery possible to regain my pride as head of the family – exhibiting another enemy of being human: ego and pride.

I did whatever was prescribed to me by medical professionals and loved ones to get back on track fast. I had a checklist of what needed to be done to achieve this goal. One-by-one, I worked on them with the top three as follows:

1) Stop medication in six months as the medication numbed my feelings. I could not be happy or sad; I needed to overcome this dependence to become a normal human having emotions.
2) Work on my soul, addressing areas such as gratitude, thankfulness, guilt, pride, anger, jealousy   ,

and selfishness. I read self-help books, attended church, and bible study as part of my soul therapy.

3) Begin interacting with people so that I could hold a conversation. I had a list of people to make connections and was thankful to secure employment with a contact, B, who incidentally was looking for people for his company. I started working on March 8, 2019, around one month after I was discharged from the hospital.

Two months on my job, my mom was diagnosed with colon cancer, stage four, and I felt helpless and guilty that I was going to lose her within one year. Every time I visited her, I could only give thanks for her unconditional love. My siblings and loved ones were very concerned that I may have a relapse due to my mom's condition. To be honest, up until May 2020, I had multiple minor regressions which happened whenever I felt fear, uncertainty, and doubt. Since then, it has never happened, and I am confident that I can handle it even if it comes again.

While working on my recovery and facing the potential loss of my mom, two other new challenges surfaced. I realised there were a lot of problems in my marriage and relationships with my children. I had spent too much focus on myself; I did not show them enough tender loving care. I was too authoritative to my wife and children, turning to use force, threats, and punishment to get my way. I was unhappy with many little things, from getting to sleep on-time to being independent that caused a lot of friction with my wife. Thankfully, we do not clash in the area of academic excellence as we both believe in having the right value system, and character is more important.

Have you ever felt jealous of someone you loved? I always had to fight my jealousy problem over my wife's better relationship with the kids, her multi-talents in many areas from the kitchen to work, and even the work that she covered for me. We consistently clashed in this area, as I demanded that she should stop working for me to find my self-worth as the head of the house.

When the church offered a marriage course, we decided to sign up and worked on our marriage, step-by-step. At the same time, we are grateful to our pastor and his wife in ministering us on parenting and marriage through our bible study. Our family relationship improved a lot through the grace and mercy of God.

In August 2019, my mom passed away, and I managed to find strength in God to go through this tough time. Every guilty thought about my mom that came into my mind was converted to giving thanks for her unconditional love.

During this period, I went through another job change to another new industry. Another contact, V, approached me to help in his new business in the medical industry. V was so observant that he knew something was not right with me when we met, he decided to offer a six-month contract with time flexibility, hoping that I can use this platform to recover at the same time. I did not have a lot of clarity at times, but it was clear that a job with time free-dom is what I needed, and I took up V's offer.

While the time freedom had helped me, this industry also brings back a lot of "traumatic memories" for me; seeing my mom's cancer treatment at the hospital and also flashes of my own experience haunts me sometimes. I do get stints of relapse from time-to-time. When I was deciding whether to quit in April 2020, I had a lot of concern about breaking the trust and kindness that this friend had shown me; this added to the stress level and relapse potential. How did I eventually manage to quit then? It was through another event that leads to where I finally found my clarity and direction.

In November 2019, I attended a Speakers Institute Boot Camp and met a classmate T, who invited me to share my testimonial at an event on overcoming toxic thoughts. This event was a public event held at a convention hall in February 2020, pre-COVID lockdown in Singapore. I was shocked when I saw an attendee (E), who was someone I knew from the technology industry. I was a bit apprehensive about sharing full details as I was worried about "losing face" in front of him. During my sharing, I did manage to "tell and testify" without hiding anything. This set me free from a lot of baggage and burden. When I can share my depression journey publicly, I have conquered my fear.

After this event, E reached out to me and introduced me to new friends and new opportunities. This happened during the COVID lockdown period, and it provided me a time to find clarity and directions. By July 2020, I could re-launch myself fully back into the technology industry with the confidence to bring more value to my partners and clients.

When I connected the dots, I understood why I had to go through this journey and would like to share these key learning points.

1) Clarity & Mindset Shape Your Vision

- Clarity of your Strength and Weakness
  - o Take up jobs that match your strength and continuously learn and unlearn to improve these strengths.
  - o Be bold to say "No" to tasks that require your weakness unless you have enough training and qualifications to perform that task.
- Clarity of your Value with the Right Mindset
  - o Instead of chasing wealth, ask ourselves what value we can offer to our employer or our clients.
  - o Always be happy to serve and be content with whatever compensation is given to you; unless you are really so "underpaid."
  - o Do not compare yourself with others.
- Body & Mind is essential, But Never Lose your Soul
  - o Manage your Desires with a Thankful Heart.
  - o Avoid making any Judgment of people in a Negative way.
  - o Always Show Gratitude and Count Your Blessings at all times.

- Keep Pride and Ego at Bay
  - Be vulnerable to admit our mistakes, learn from it, and move on.
  - Seek forgiveness from people that we have offended during a conflict.

2) Discipline & Persistence Create Your Future
- Be Disciplined in taking the Right Action
  - There is a formula for everything. Whether it is losing weight, recovery from illness, or pursuing a dream, always ensure that you do not stop taking the right action.
- Stay Focused with your Dream that Resonates within your Heart
  - Do not look outward and deviate your attention as the grass on the other side always seemed greener.
  - Continue to learn, acquire new knowledge, and seek coaching/mentor and stay with this dream.
- Keep Running
  - Whether a Big Step or a small step, keep moving.
- Remember to be "Disciplined" to include "Downtime" in your Journey
  - Even systems need downtime to rest and recover.
  - Rest provides us the stamina to execute discipline and persistence.

I used to think that once success is achieved, we can retire and do whatever we want with that financial freedom. Today, I believe that we are here to serve and make the world a better place for everyone. This experience has helped me redefine my vision and have become a great believer in my future. I hope you have enjoyed my story and can define your vision and create your future.

--------------------- For my own records -------------------

Acknowledgments & Thank You:

Special Thanks to God for his Grace and Mercy

My Family & Love Ones for their enduring love & support:

- My dear wife, Linda; our lovely daughters Ying & Xuan; our adorable son Teng
- My late parents; Sisters Eileen & Jenny, Brothers Ronald, Luke & YJ
- Uncle Low and Family, Auntie Lau and Family

My Friends & Business Partners their forgiveness and opportunities that help us grow

- TS, CS, CH, B, V, T & E

Pastors, Brothers & Sisters @ Grace Baptist Ministries

Other friends not mentioned in this story: Jeffrey, Wilson, Richard, Kelvin, Adrian, Eugene and the Fathers Group @ my son's school.

All other people whom I met along the journey, a big thank you for being part of this story.

About Vinson Chua

Startup | Business Development | Speaker

"Clarity and Mindset Shape your Vision.

Discipline and Persistence Create your Future"

Profession:

- Co-Founder of Technology Startup Lumani
- Green Cooling Advocate With EcoLine Solar

Passion:

- Environmental Sustainability
- Physical & Mental Well-Being

Community Work:

- Founder of Father @ White Sands Primary School
- Human Environment Wellness Standard Advocate

Personal:

- Married with 3 Lovely Kids

LinkedIn - www.linkedin.com/in/chua-kong-hee-vinson

Facebook - https://www.facebook.com/vinson.chua.1/

BENEFITS OF SIMPLIFYING YOUR LIFE

By Chrissy G. Tasker

We are wired with a special purpose to be what we are.

The ability to choose gave us the choice to decode better experience in order

To better ourself so that we can serve our fellowmen.

– Scientist Gregg Brenden

If you have been thinking of how to simplifies your life lately, it is likely you are seeking some change in your life, whether it be freedom from a type of physical or mental clutter.

But, why do we crave simplicity?

To find the answer, we need to dive deeper into the benefits of a simplified life and what it means to seek it.

Clarity

Clarity may sound intangible, but I think we can all put our finger on what it means to us.

Clarity of mind is when the fog clears, when you are able to make decisions without being weighed down by your worries, overthinking every detail before coming to a final conclusion.

To some, clarity of mind is about peace. A feeling of transparency or purity in your thoughts that helps you to move forward. Clarity is something within our minds and hearts that helps us to see clearly and take a fresh look at our lives. Without a sense of clarity in ourselves, we can't have clarity in our lives as a whole[3].

Mental clarity may seem hard to achieve. If you've ever laid awake at night thinking about tomorrow's work, the kid's schoolwork what needs doing around the house or worrying about the people you love, you will understand what I mean.

It can be difficult to dig through the myriad of thoughts we have on a daily basis to find those that are clear and straightforward. Imagine your brain like your internet browser. Sometimes we open a new tab and leave it open, not actively using it but knowing we'll need it again

---

[3] Further reading – Steven Shuster, *Clear Your Mind* (2017).

soon. Now imagine you do this with 20, 50, 100s of new tabs. You will struggle to find the tab you need.

This is what your mind is like when you are lacking clarity. Every time you think of something new you need to do, a task not yet completed, you open a new tab in your mind and store it until it is finished. This goes for the big things – long term goals, important tasks, dreams and aspirations – as well as for the little or everyday items – short term goals like cleaning, cooking and errands. With so many tabs open it is understandable that you can't sort through the mess and find the most important pieces of information.

You may want to prioritise those big things and get them finished, but in order to do that you need the other tabs open too. Before you know, you are overwhelmed by items, clogging up your mind. As the mind begins to clog, so does your soul, and your sense of calm. Just as a computer system can't run an infinite number of processes, your mind can't juggle an infinite number of tasks. You shouldn't chastise yourself for struggling to find what you need, prioritise tasks and cross things off your to-do list when you have so much going on in your mind. Moreover, you can't expect to be at peace with yourself when you have so much clouding your mind.

In his article on *Medium*, Thomas Oppong calls this "mental chatter" – a constant back and forth between your brain and its own thoughts that can lead to an unquiet mind.

Oppong attributes this to the amount of time we spend in our heads instead of being in the moment; he says, "Many people spend more time in their heads than they need to — 80 percent of the time. This habit creates a default background of anxiety, stress, preoccupation and less time enjoying the moment."[4]

That feeling of constant thoughts swirling through your mind can be anxiety-inducing; after all, we're stuck with our own minds 24/7 whether we like it or not.

Mental clarity doesn't have to be hard to achieve – by being more mindful of our own thoughts, quieting the mind with journaling and meditation and finding gratitude and acceptance in life are all ways to increase our sense of mental clarity and stop feeling so overwhelmed[5].

If you feel that your mind is becoming bogged down by tasks, think again of the computer analogy. Which tabs will you keep? Do you need to worry about everything simultaneously, or can you take some time to sort through and prioritise your thoughts?

As you continue through this book, you will find that the answer becomes yes – you can learn how to find mental clarity by quieting your mind with purposeful and targeted stillness.

---

[5] For further reading see Richard Gilpin, *Mindfulness for Unravelling Anxiety: Finding Calm and Clarity in Uncertain Times* (2016)

Reduce Stress

Stress has become part of daily life for a lot of us. Did you know that 74% of people in the UK in 2017 reported feeling 'overwhelmed or unable to cope'? This number only increased for millennials – 83% of 18-24 year olds said this compared to 65% of people aged over 55. There are lots of ways that we can successfully reduce our stress, but once we get on this path, it can be difficult to change our habits and lifestyles to find more calm and less pressure.

For a lot of us, as we strive towards success, we may start to feel that "work" and "stress" are synonymous. Whether you find your work life stressful, are burdened by an endless to-do list or can never seem to get on top of the housework, in the modern world we seem to find ways to stress ourselves out. The pressures of modern society are only exacerbated by a culture of one-upmanship – as an increasingly globalised world opens up new career opportunities and easier communication, it can be difficult to resist comparing ourselves to others, seeking more in our careers and presenting ourselves as productive and up-and-coming. All of this extra pressure leads to extra stress and stress leads to being strung out – in work and in our personal lives.

You may be asking – why do we feel stress in the first place?

Stress, however awful it makes us feel, did have a biological purpose for our ancestors. When we come into contact with something that we can't control, perceive as dangerous or know to have hurt us in the past, our body triggers stress hormones to prepare us for the "fight or flight" reaction. Sometimes, it can be a kick up the backside (remember that feeling of propulsion after you've procrastinated a task too long?), our body's way of making sure we power through difficult situations. If stress is short term, it can have this desired effect[6].

The landscape modern humans find ourselves in just doesn't need stress in the same way our ancestors did, and unfortunately, that means stress has become a knee-jerk and often harmful reaction to our daily lives. To quote comedienne Ruby Wax's *A Mindfulness Guide for the Frazzled*, "we're unaware that part of our brains still plays by the rules of 500 million years ago."[7]

Accepting that this is part of our biology is just one step towards reducing our stress. It is also important to know exactly what stress does to our bodies because of this hormonal reaction so that we can combat it and the negative health benefits it ushers in. You can acknowledge your stress whilst also striving to banish it[8]. Here are just some of

---

[6] "Stress" on *Mental Health Foundation* [accessed 15.6.20 - https://www.mentalhealth.org.uk/a-to-z/s/stress#:~:text=When%20we%20encounter%20stress%2C%20our,appropriate%2C%20or%20even%20beneficial%20reaction.]

[7] Ruby Wax, *A Mindfulness Guide for the Frazzled* (2016)

[8] Emily and Amelia Nagoski's *Burnout: The secret to solving the stress cycle* (2019) separates the idea of "stressor" (something which

the physical and mental symptoms that can be linked to stress[9]:

Physical

- Dizziness
- Headaches and migraines
- Muscle tension/pain
- Chest pains
- Fatigue
- Stomach ulcers
- Change in libido
- Digestion issues
- Trouble sleeping
- Overeating or undereating

Mental

- Anxiety
- Depression
- Restlessness
- Lack of motivation
- Feeling overwhelmed
- Irritability
- Difficulty concentrating

____

causes stress) and the "stress" itself. Sometimes cutting out the "stressors" doesn't solve the stress itself. You need to go deeper to s

- Constantly worrying
- The problem with stress is that it builds up – often we repress the first few issues that are stressing us out which out leads to a domino effect further down the line.
- Is reducing stress possible when you work full time?
- Absolutely! In fact, now more than ever there is an abundance of support and guidance for people who are feeling overwhelmed by their work or home life.
- Here are some dos and don'ts for reducing stress:

DO:

- Talk to friends of family. Create a safe space to share how you are feeling.
- Take control. Acknowledging that you are struggling is the first step in reducing your stress.
- Make space for down time in your life. Mark off an hour, an afternoon, a day, a weekend to have complete down time.
- Embrace time management. Procrastination is a difficult habit to kick, but try to remember that it will only lead to more stress in the long run.

DON'T:

- Don't take on everything at once. Be in control of your schedule. Break projects down into small, achievable targets.

- Don't focus on the things you cannot change. Accept that you can't change them and focus on the things you can change.
- Don't be afraid to ask for help. Other people can help to reduce your mental load, whether it is through a comforting conversation or by taking on some of your tasks themselves.

Become more productive

It may seem axiomatic to say that when you are burnt out from stress and overthinking, you cannot achieve your maximum productivity, but it is a fact that many people grapple with.

Graham Alcott's book *How to be a Productivity Ninja* outlines that you need to accept that you can't do everything, but when we are conscious of our work we can be more productive: "we *are* ultimately in control and [...] we do ultimately have enough hours in the day to get important stuff done (you'll notice I didn't just say get 'everything' done.)"[10]

Ask yourself – why do I struggle to complete my to-do list? How can I be more productive without becoming more stressed?

The answer lies in clarity and stress reduction: to put it simply, you cannot increase your productivity without first

---

[10] Graham Alcott, *How to be a Productivity Ninja* (2012).

addressing your mental clutter and stress-levels. As Alcott says, you need to priorities tasks, but you also need to seek moments where you can priorities your attention.

Have you ever had a feeling of continuous productive momentum? That powerful feeling of pushing through your to-do list can only come when you have focus. To gain focus on a particular task, you need clarity of mind and prioritisation.

Another technique that simplifies your productivity is a reward system. Humans, like all animals, have an in-built sense of completion. The buzz that we get from completing something can lead into a flow of productivity. Try organising your to-do lists with small tasks first. When you blow through these easily, the momentum can often carry you through into other seemingly bigger tasks.

Using mindfulness to become more productive is as simple as three steps. These six steps may seem difficult now, but as we push further into this book and what it means to find stillness within yourself, you will find it easier to push for more productivity.

- Step 1 – clear your mind of tasks that aren't relevant to the current situation. If you're at work, write down the domestic or personal tasks that are weighing on your mind and put them aside. Having a post-it note, small note book, notepad on Mobile device. I personally use google keep on My phone devise with these points on it will make it easier for you to remove them from your current thoughts.

- Step 2 - List with tick box work best for me. Being able to physically ticked it off give me a visual confirmation and sense of achievement to let me know I am on the right path.

- Step 3 – dig deeper into what is making you feel stressed about the task. Can you remove some of the stress by doing a smaller task first? Try tackling the most daunting part of your to-do list straight away so that the stress doesn't build up over time.

- Step 4 – learn to capitalise on your moments of greatest focus. If you are feeling sluggish, take a break and come back to your task later, or move onto something else until you can clear your mind and refocus.

- Step 5 -In many occasion, when I felt overwhelmed by the incomplete task list in front of me, the universe usually sent a message to nerd me to do something else and return to the list later.

- Step 6- Very often I am being reminded by my faithful four-legged friend, Reggie, a walk outdoors with the fresh air will help to clear my head and in turn able to see things in a different perspective and return to the desk to produce a better result.

No matter how overwhelmed you feel right now, you can reduce your stress and take control of your life. Consider what kind of work-life balance you would like in your ideal reality and make progress towards that. Do you need to remove something from your schedule? Is there a change you can make in your home life that will mean not doing a job that stresses you out? Can you lean on someone else in your life to help you?

All of these factors will go into turning down the heat on your daily life and moving forward to a calmer lifestyle.

May light and love be with you.

About Chrissy Tasker

Chrissy G. Tasker is an Inspirational speaker, Number one bestselling author, Leader, and a Certified Public Speaker. She is the award winner for The Most Inspiring Women of Our Time 2016, Award winner for Women Entrepreneur BY KPMG 2014 and many time Million Dollar Round Table's Award winner in the Prestige Insurance industries.

Her passion for collaboration and seeking alliances lead her to many of her success in her business venture. Chrissy Tasker has spent years getting under the bonnet of some of the world's renowned organisation seeking alliances with different companies and business owners. She believes how collaboration can bring together ambitious individuals to become more than the sum of their parts.

She is the founder of The World is So Big Publishing and run **Author Syndicate Academy**, an online course that teaches students to publish their book in 90 days.

She deeply concerns for the welfare for the underprivileged children, and
she is now the ambassador speaker for The Children Society Charity Organisation.

Book by Chrissy G. Tasker

How to be a Great Podcast Guest

Stillness in My Soul

The Power of Collaboration

Facebook - https://www.facebook.com/chrissyauction

LinkedIn - https://www.linkedin.com/in/chrissy-tasker-1230111b/

Website: Chrissytasker.com

WHICH WOLF WILL YOU FEED

By Angela Mah

It is late in the night. I looked at my dog, Sweetie, enjoying her sleep with her nightly (and mighty) snore as she went into the lullaby. She is now 13-years-old and entering the sunset of her canine life. For the pet owners, we know what this means – we are losing precious time every single day. It is the nature of life, yet it is a helpless feeling that over-whelms me from time-to-time – looking at her in deep slumber, such sweet innocence, and total surrender. I often wonder if Sweetie knows what is ahead of her. Perhaps she does, and maybe she chooses to relish every moment until she is called up to the Rainbow Bridge? I had to pull my hands away from her warm body, less she feels the bittersweet emotions starting to stir within me.

My mind started to drift back involuntarily to 2013 – a year that was to be the beginning of an exciting phase of my life, yet ironically would also turn out to be the beginning of the lowest point as well. Such a strange feeling with the cocktail of euphoria and despair blended together.

October 2013, fresh out of a sabbatical, I was given a rare opportunity to embark on an exciting international assignment to Mumbai, India. Having taken on a stint in the United States some years before, I was all ready for another adventure, which I believed would not only showcase my experience and agility, it would also bring value to the business. The voyager in me needed nothing else – the mission to add value was too attractive to say no. Armed with the call of duty and my two beloved dogs, Snowy and Pearl – Woohoo India – here I come!

Just before the relocation, something strange triggered in me – jitters got the better of me, and I suddenly started questioning my judgment and decision. What if my new colleagues do not take well to me? What if I fail to accomplish what I set out to do? What if I was biting off more than I can chew? What if I fall flat on my face? It didn't help that sensationalized horror stories of the country kept playing in my head. The more I tried to get a grip over myself, the more the shadow of fear loomed over me.

As I went through a mental checklist of the pros and cons of the assignment, while I knew there were many upsides to the opportunity, the fear of the unknown, especially the prospect of being all alone in a foreign country, fear of failure, and judgment, et cetera, was so clear and present. Have you ever had times when you told yourself to snap the thoughts out of your head, yet they seemed to churn faster and faster, so much so that they appeared to be like stubborn flies, refusing to swat off your face? For a person who was known to be sensible, confident, and in control, I felt that I could not speak or confide in anyone. I felt like a failure for that, like a failure even before the challenge started! I felt dizzy from the series of "What ifs" that swirled like a whirlpool within me.

Was I putting the self-manufactured fallacies in my head? Once I was able to acknowledge all these fears and resist the waves of emotions, something different happened in me. Instead of focusing on the negatives, I found myself questioning how sure I was that "the worst-case" would genuinely happen, asking how to make the best of my fears. I found that where we train our mind to focus, our energy flows in that direction. That was when something magical happened – instead of spending my time and energy fearing for the worst to come true, I was able to focus on how to materialize the upside. Slowly, the waves of noise and frenzy in my head (and more so, my heart) began to ebb as I put together a strategy to prepare myself for the exciting adventure ahead of me. This new-found mindset not only helped me stub out the self-doubt, but it was also in the days to come, the key to overcoming the challenges that would be unleashed upon me.

As I started to settle down in Mumbai, the initial period of the new assignment was tumultuous. Despite my best attempts, I had difficulty connecting with my new colleagues, and the spicy food was less than helpful. My mind kicked into gear to find ways to appreciate the culture better, develop a support network while juggling with taking care of my two beloved dogs. I engaged a coach to guide me through some of the challenges at work, and to this day, I remain grateful that he enabled me to learn so much through our interactions. With all the support, my strategy to integrate into my newly-adopted country began paying dividends, and I started enjoying the beauty of India and the challenge of the assignment. The lessons learned were so empowering that I am a coach today because I want to pay it forward to help another person unleash his/her potential.

Just when things started to bear fruit, the next wave of disaster hit me from out of nowhere. Snowy seemed to be out of sorts and would yelp in pain when she was picked up. After consulting three different vets, on 15 February 2015, I was told that Snowy had salivary gland carcinoma. I could not believe my ears – how could she suddenly contract cancer out of the blue and have only less than three months left? I picked up the phone to consult the vet in Singapore, and it was confirmed that chemotherapy would not help. It would be best not to put Snowy through more pain than she was already suffering from. This was like a death sentence, and all I could do was work with the oncologist on a palliative plan. It was heart-wrenching to see her change from a lively girl to a bag of bones. As things began breaking down, all I could do was put up a brave front, continuing to discharge my responsibilities at work, while spending weekends with Snowy at the pet radiation center before taking the flight out for business the next day.

Was I fearful of the days ahead? Definitely! The clock seemed to tick faster. I was knocked off balance with so many things to juggle. While the crisis remained the same, I realized (again) that how I decided to put a meaning to all these would affect my response. To borrow the ancient Cherokee story: all of us have two wolves inside us, always at battle with each other. One is the good wolf that represents the positive – optimism, hope, and resilience. The other is the bad wolf, which means the negative in us – our fears, insecurities, anger, and sadness, amongst others. The wolf that we decide to feed will become the wolf of our life. In this case, the quicker and the more I fed the good wolf, the more I will be able to focus my mind on solutions and finding ways to enjoy the time I had left with Snowy. The pain and sadness that I was losing Snowy with each day did not go away. However, each day I had with her was spent with gratitude and much love. In fact, to this day, it is with fond memories whenever I find myself recounting my stint in India, whenever I see her pictures. God had blessed Snowy with seven months instead of the three months. Words cannot express the gratitude I had with this extended time.

While Snowy ultimately succumbed to cancer, God sent me angels in the form of supportive colleagues and boss, the oncologist, my coach, driver, helper, and so many more to name. I could not imagine how much more difficult it would have been if these angels were not planted in my life at that time.

Six months after Snowy passed away, it was Pearl's turn to contract cancer. By this time, not only did I have the experience to know who to turn to for treatment, I was then able to start creating good days and fond memories with her much earlier. We went to the beach often, Pearl was always with me on the ride to the office and back, bought her more toys to take her mind off the discomfort, and even celebrated her birthday with a homemade cake. By this time, I decided that it was time to look after Pearl and my needs. I resigned from my job, and I was glad Pearl managed to come back to Singapore.

Fast forward to 2020 – Sweetie is starting to lose her vision and her hearing. But guess what? I am so glad that she continues to have a quality life, that I am in a position to readjust my priorities to be here for her. I focused on the many days of blessings and joy that Sweetie brought to my life. I know I am much more prepared for this stage of her life, and I will hold her paw until it is time to say goodbye. We will create great memories with each day we have together.

Life will continue to throw us a smorgasbord of challenges and blessings, and perhaps some of you may even be experiencing your fair share of hard knocks as we speak. I hope to share some lessons learned as inspiration to weather the unfamiliar terrains:

Lesson #1: determine your Why – do I have a compelling reason for doing what I am doing? The human spirit is unbreakable. We must have a passion and perhaps even a calling – if we find it a struggle to determine the compelling reason to march on, maybe we may need to question if it is even worth investing our energy into it? Perhaps that may not be our Why?

Lesson #2: The amount of time and energy we have is finite. Therefore, how should we optimize our time and energy? Would we rather spend the time agonizing on the problem and inconveniences, or would we instead channel our energy to overcome the roadblocks and perhaps create a new trajectory?

Lesson #3: Learn to build mental resilience by challenging and reframing our mind – instead of "what **now**," turn the situation around to ask the question, "what's **next**?" It may seem a deliberate action in the beginning; however, when we do this often enough, you will be amazed that subsequent mindset switches will be increasingly easier and intuitive,

Lesson #4: This, too, shall pass – with each wave of a challenge, a new wave of blessings will follow. Perhaps we wish that we did not have to suffer the inconveniences, yet perhaps that is to prepare us for bigger and better things to come? For every sunset, there will be a sunrise. The challenges may be real, yet, it is often a matter of perspective that will help us see the silver lining, and in turn, allow us to respond to them differently.

As for me, I am filled with gratitude , not so much for the anguish (I will be crazy to suggest that), but for the strength I have developed, to know that the human spirit is unbreakable. At the end of the day, the wolf that we feed will be the master of our life. So, my friends, my wish and encouragement for you is choose wisely, *very wisely*.

About Angel Mah

Angela Mah has more than 30 years of diverse regional experience in human resource management in the MNCs in the medical/pharmaceutical, chemical, consulting, agriculture technology, renewable energy and engineering sectors. Angela works with business stakeholders and leaders to curate business-centric HR strategies and interventions to high performance culture. She has helped numerous multi-national organizations set up efficient and effective human capital management solutions to enhance the employee experience, build resilience and develop talents to achieve business outcomes.

Angela is a strong believer and champion of an individual's potential. In the recent five years, Angela coaches and mentors business leaders and high-potentials to develop their leadership skills using evidence based solutions focus approach. Angela is a certified Corporate Coach through her association with WABC, WBECS and ICF.

On top of these, Angela is also an Entrepreneur and mentor.

https://www.linkedin.com/in/angela-mah-a5892aab

SKILLS THAT THRILL

By Dr. Anita

"A smooth sea never made a skilful mariner"
English proverb

"I am on a plane at the moment and travelling. Thank you for your message. I viewed your profile. Wow!"

I was ecstatic to read his reply. It was August 2018, and I had just attended his half-day workshop in Mumbai. I had left the venue without registering for his 3-day boot camp to be held at a later date. Soon after, I went for my swim, and my inner guidance kicked in, nudging me to reach out to him. So, I sent him a text message.

"Hello, something shifted inside me after hearing your talk, and I wish to embark on being a speaker and an author. Is the boot camp offer made at the venue still available?"

Little did I know that he would be a significant influence and mentor in my life. He was Sam Cawthorn, CEO, Speakers Institute, Australia.

Exactly one year before this serendipitous event, I had exited from my full-time job as a Professor in Transfusion Medicine. For sixteen years, I was at the helm of a large blood bank with a bone marrow transplant facility. I had handed over the resignation letter to my hospital director, as I realised I had a calling, and it was not in this place. I left the job without talking about it to a single person in my life. I knew people would think I was at my wit's end to leave a secure job and position vied by many medical professionals. I was excelling in academics and bestowed with best paper awards at the annual National conferences of our medical fraternity.

This led to my selection for giving scientific presentations at international conferences in the USA for three consecutive years and in Dubai and Bangkok. Tata's is a substantial and trusted brand in India, and I was employed at their top cancer hospital affiliated with the central government. The pay and the perks were incredible, along with recognition, if you were academically oriented and doing pioneering research. The satisfaction derived from implementing one's professional knowledge into practical applications for the betterment of humanity is an incomparable driving force to give your peak performance. I embarked on 'first-time-ever' projects with my bright students. We initiated platelet donation drives for students in various colleges in Mumbai by collaborating with the renowned NGOs (*Nargis Dutt Cancer Foundation*). We imported the latest platelet additive solutions from France (*Maco-pharma Co. Ltd*) and conducted successful experiments to increase the shelf life of platelets from the existing five days to seven days. Both of these projects were awarded best paper awards for their novelty, execution, and results. I felt contentment as I had made apt use of the resources, making an honest and dedicated contribution to Science.

However, I was not the one who would ignore the silent whispers of my soul. Life is cyclical in nature, and it is best to get off the bi'cycle' when there is compelling evidence that a cycle has ended. I intuitively sensed the urge to make a decision to foray into the unknown by letting go of my identity, colleagues, and current professional environment. Group consciousness, whether in a small social setting or country, can make or break you. I had to be discerning and avoid distractions generated by other's opinions. It was as if the Universe had brought me to the edge of a cliff and tested my ability to trust in the Divine.

It took me three years to plan my exit from this hospital setting. It was a success trap, but a trap nevertheless. The signs and synchronicities I encountered were unmistakable and occurred daily. I maintained a journal to keep track of the messages and study their patterns. These signs from the Universe were like breadcrumbs to follow; a trail when on an adventure. I had read it as a child in novels like *Famous Five* and *Nancy Drew*. But this was happening to me in real life. And who would believe it? But I had to believe in myself. I soon realised that these meaningful events were inherently the promptings of my soul. The soul is a reservoir of all the skills and experiences from our past lifetimes. Tapping into its innate wisdom can unravel your hidden gifts. No one knew my soul's path better than me.

It was August 2017, and the soft whisper turned into a scream. It was time to take that leap of faith. I jumped! But there was no landing in sight. I persuaded myself 'If you can imagine it, you can achieve it.' And, thus began my transition toward my new life. My greatest challenge had just begun. As the high momentum of the daily hospital routine stopped, I felt as if I had been pulled off of a hamster wheel. I had to change my state of 'doing' to a state of 'being.' I had to understand the difference between Aloneness and Loneliness.

The first is the presence of oneself, while the second is the absence of another. Buddha's teachings 'Be a light unto yourself' reverberated in my mind. The world was functioning in the same way as before, but my reality had undergone a quantum shift. My ego took a beating, as I had attached my entire life to my identity as a professional. It was 'Who I was.' – and suddenly, I wasn't. That is when I questioned, 'Who Am I?' This is the most important question that a spiritual seeker can ask in the pursuit of self-discovery. Even though my spiritual quest had begun at the tender age of 15 through meditation, this was a next level transition. Mindfulness practices had helped me tremendously to bring focus into my life to survive the trials of the medical profession. But to be asked by my higher self to let go of everything in my current reality tested my inner spiritual strength to its limits. My outward journey had stopped and given birth to an inward journey. It was scary when it appeared that I was stripped of my worldly achievements. I say appeared because I could not see the big picture just yet. It was a precious moment and one that was full of poignancy. Just like a drop of water may tremble before it falls off a leaf, I, too, was on the edge between the known and the unknown. It was a time of letting go, allowing any sadness within to rise but not trying to hold onto it.

As I walked for the last time out of the hospital feeling remorse, a message caught my eye. It said, 'Leaving an X-rated life behind.' It was a sign that much better things were in the near future. This job had fed my ego. Now it was time to feed my soul. Little did I know that it was a detour to a cherished destination!

Being ready, I committed myself to embark on my new adventure. Creativity begins where the survival instinct ends. The barricade that withholds us in life is our own mental prison and belief systems. As I now had ample time on my hands to do what I wished to, I asked myself:

- What are my passions, talents, and gifts that I have not had the opportunity to explore before?
- What fills my heart with joy and makes me feel energised, even after doing it for long hours?

- What makes me get up in the morning with enthusiasm and brings a spring to my step throughout the day?
- What would I do if money was not a constraint?
- What will give me the freedom to work as and when I want to?

I had to answer these questions honestly and with authenticity. My second inning of life had begun, and I refused to be a bystander, watching my life go by from the sidelines. The only limitation in life is the one that resides within our own being. I knew I had to roll up my sleeves and get into the groove if I wanted to achieve my dreams. I had to become the 'Star' of my life movie, and that meant participating fully in whatever came in my path. I incorporated the following into my daily practice.

- **Being in the Now moment** and not reminiscing about the past or lingering too far into the future. I had to co-create with the Universe, moment-to-moment, as the entire plan is never laid out before us and our free will choices determine the outcome. All of this is easier said than done because, as humans, we have a mental, emotional, spiritual, physical, and ethereal body that creates confusion if not balanced appropriately.
- **Awareness** is critical when learning new concepts or polishing one's existing gifts. Knowledge through books imparts a solid foundation when embarking into unknown territories. The mindset with which one

approaches the day-to-day activities determines the output gained at the end of each day.

- **Learning** from mentors who have already walked this path and formulated the tools to make it easier for the newbies is a wise decision. They are our guides who can shine a light in the darkest moments. Attending workshops and training sessions with experts can help in gaining insight and understand the ropes of the game, no matter what the subject.

- **'Know thyself'** is a spiritual requirement for gaining wisdom and may compel one to retreat from family and friends, even though it may hurt their sentiments. Going within and disconnecting from the matrix can bring newer perspectives to our human existence and recognition of our soul's essence and true spirituality.

- **Networking** with like-minded people who stand by you during tough times and also having an accountability partner can keep you engaged to do your best. As I was going through a spiritual awakening, and none around me were experiencing the same, I joined international groups on the Internet and bonded within these support groups. This networking helped me to move forward on my path in real-time without self-doubts about myself. I realised that having supernatural experiences is not 'going crazy' even though some may ridicule it out of ignorance or intentional spite. But each soul's journey is different; hence there needn't be any judgment if there are obvious differences.

- **Playfulness** and creating from a happy place within is as important as having sunshine after a rainy day. It works like an elixir to energise and speed up the manifestation process. The results that can materialise from a high vibrational state of being will far exceed what was embarked upon from a place of sadness and victim mentality.

- **Physical exercise** in the form of walking, jogging, or swimming helps as our miracle bodies work like a finely tuned musical instrument when functioning at its peak. Inner alignment has to be achieved daily, as the blockages we harbour in our chakras (energy centres) are reflected back upon us in our outer reality.

- **Decluttering** our lives of toxic energies, whether they be in the form of personal addictions or high conflict people giving unsolicited advice, goes a long way to get crystal clear clarity about our direction in life. Managing time wisely to make it productive, without unnecessary distractions, can help to develop a laser focus toward one's goals.

- **Negative programming** of our brains through social media, TV, and newspapers needs to be curtailed if we are to rid ourselves of old beliefs and harmful patterns. Progression is not possible while being in a regressive mind frame, which happens if we allow ourselves to be ruled by outdated societal constructs.

- **Saying no** to the naysayers is vital when you are guided to go down a less trodden path. They cannot see nor hold your vision; hence your own personal conviction about what you are creating is crucial to the success on your soul's path, which is as unique as the snowflakes in nature. To do groundbreaking work, we need to make a dent in the current reality and form our own codes of conduct suitable to the current scenarios and the new world order being established.

- **Patience** and being in tune with the Universal flow of life can reap rich rewards. We begin to realise that we are part of a giant jigsaw puzzle on earth, and all the co-operative components need to fall into place for any manifestation to reach fruition. Trust in a higher power and develop a strong inner, knowing that this unseen force works best when we get out of the way!

- **Inspired actions** should be taken on a regular basis as they are proof that you are on course with your destiny. Events and outcomes effortlessly progress when your motivation to make changes arises from your core being and the promptings of your soul.

After a year of intense inner work, the Universe geared into action for me. Yes, you matter. Each one of us matters because we carry the particular skill sets that are unique to us and completes the grand scheme of things in this world. Divine intelligence is pure energy and penetrates all matter to reveal the hidden mysteries. Signals emanated through us in the form of thoughts and feelings, magnetises events that are meant to come into our reality. The subconscious mind and our inherent self-talk throughout the day determine the quality of our experiences. High vibrational thoughts will produce joy, compassion, generosity, bliss, harmony, and love for all of life. Only love is real, and once the layers of illusion are seen for what they are, we shall not be able to unsee what is once seen. The world is waking up rapidly, and many are on the fast-track to spiritual ascension. Whether we upscale to the 5th dimension realm or remain stuck in this dense 3rd dimension realm will depend on the choices we make in the 'Now' moment. Humans have free will, and we determine the course of our destiny. The higher realms represent the existence of effortless ease, and manifestation happens as if by magic. Creative visualisation of our desired outcome will bring it to us if all other components of the intended desire are in the highest good of all. Hence, being mindful of our thought patterns is crucial, and those individuals who have mastered this art will get to taste the beauty of oneness with all that is. Decades of meditation practice made it easier for me to stay connected to my higher guidance even through the existing challenges. I did not meddle with the 'how' of my goals. I focused on the feeling of deep satisfaction of having it in my life, even though it was physically not yet tangible. Sure enough, the blockages in my path dissolved. Abundance in all areas of life is our birth right. The heart is the seat of creation, moving forward into this golden age of Aquarius. The heart's intelligence is 5,000 times more magnetically stronger than the brain. Become a 'brave heart' today!

Receptivity is an inner state of being wherein your own inner blockages do not hamper the process of evolution. I was open to learning and growing every day. I came across workshop advertisements conducted by skilled mentors, and I responded without hesitation. In one of these interactive workshops, we were given white card papers, magazines for cut-outs, and sketch pens. We were asked to make a vision board in 45 minutes. It was like setting a ball rolling, and the energy started gaining momentum in my life. Within the next 15 days, I was on a prestigious platform giving a talk in the presence of an elite crowd. I met new soulmates who were catalysts for my greatest transformation. Proximity is power, and I was blessed to meet meditation masters, success coaches, energy healers, transformation experts, and spiritual gurus who were key toward my blossoming into the best version of me. I felt as if I had a whirlwind romance with my destiny.

As I plunged headfirst into honing my skills, I realised that my energy was consistently high, as I loved what I was doing. The Universe senses your energy. And I was broadcasting the best electromagnetic waves into the quantum field where all possibilities exist. I felt passionate as I connected with those who were on the same wavelength as me. My commitment to evolve spiritually took me into unprecedented territories. My psychic abilities developed, further clearing my *Ajna chakra* (third eye), and the layers of illusion started to disappear, making way to deeper insights. I was doing readings for people through divination tools like Tarot and helping them to understand and solve their complex life situations. Clearing the aura and energy around my physical body enabled me to do the same for those around me and even perform distant healing on people in far off places. Group meditations and breathwork helped me in emotional detoxification and to align my body, mind, and soul. I had been initiated into feeling deep Divine Love within my soul. Love energy can transmute all lower energies – love fuels creativity. As I embodied this love throughout the day, it brought me a realisation about the miracles and healings possible with this energy. My ego-self dissolved, and my soul was now in the driver's seat. Decision-making was easier as the mind did not interfere with the truth of my heart. I found myself relaxed and yet more alert than ever!

My new soul tribe became my motivation to be my best self. Some became my accountability partners to practice speaking and writing short stories regularly. My success coaches mentored me to keep a 360-degree view on all aspects of life: physical, emotional, spiritual, financial, and social so that I did not lose sight of the many facets that go on to make me feel whole and complete. It isn't easy to measure success. How *you* feel about each area of your life defines your failure and success.

I started my webpage, where I regularly updated my activities. It was like a mind movie of the new reality I had entered. It kept me focused and gave me a taste of the human ability to co-create with the Universe. The constant encouragement from my online supporters empowered me and fuelled my knowing that I was on the right path and leading a purposeful life.

It is important to compare a vision board with an achievement board to celebrate each small success. Today, I can connect the dots and see the deeper truths to the unfoldment in my journey. I found myself reminiscing about an episode that happened soon after quitting my job. My mother was admitted in critical condition for diabetes complications. Intensive care units, long nights, doctor consultations, and uncertainties were part of my existence for months. On one such day, as I sat in the lobby contemplating about the direction in which my life was headed, I saw a message on a board **'Skills that Thrill.'** When a message is meant for me, it resonates so deeply that any doubt or analysis vanishes. All that remains is faith and a calm acceptance in Source energy that is guiding me at all times. I had released my past life choices, but in turn, I had created space for new possibilities of being a clairvoyant, spiritual teacher, energy healer, speaker, and author, which complimented my training as a doctor. No learning is ever wasted.

Now, when a person approaches me with a problem, I view him/her as a whole person (Mind, Body, Soul) and can offer unique solutions by combining my scientific and spiritual knowledge. My approach assists them in overcoming their personal challenges in health, relationships, and career as they are all inter-related in the bigger scheme of things. Treating the bodily symptoms with drugs and not addressing the root cause of the ailments is a failure of modern medicine. Ancient wisdom viewed humans as having healing capabilities that have been numbed by rampant usage of pharmaceuticals. For example, treating clinical depression without addressing its root cause is akin to ignoring the proverbial 'elephant in the room.' Drugs cure the symptom, which is the 'tip of the iceberg,' while ancient science acknowledges the presence of the entire submerged iceberg!

It was brought to my realisation that it was time to merge western science with spiritual wisdom and think outside the box. It helped me to embark on a new path that is in tune with the current changing times. From a medical doctor, I transformed into being a wholistic doctor & healer.

Transitions in life are not to be feared. It may be a necessary detour for finding beautiful treasures which may otherwise be missed. When life throws a curveball, explore the possibility that 'Not all curves are dangerous!'

My message

Life happens in cycles, and transitions are inevitable

Patience and Trust are key to navigate through uncertain times

Be equipped with tools to optimise your situation

Know that it is a test of your spiritual strength

Learn and connect with those who have experienced it and succeeded

Never give up as your life is an adventure

Be the alchemist that you are meant to be on this planet.

About Dr. Anita

Dr Anita is a doctor (MBBS, MD, DPB, DIT), a gifted clairvoyant and tarot expert, certified energy healer, speaker and author. She has been a professor in the medical profession for two decades. She transitioned to healing and empowering people through an integrative Body - Mind - Soul approach. She provides unique solutions to people facing varying life challenges, be it relationships, career, health, new ventures, etc through her divination tools as she believes she is a channel for Divine Source energy and considers herself as a 'messenger'. She is the recipient of many best paper awards at National conferences and has presented scientific papers at international conferences. She resides in Mumbai, India and can be contacted at anitatendulkar@gmail.com. Her business page and testimonials are available at https://www.facebook.com/stargalaxy1111

You can connect with her at _anitatendulkar@gmail.com_

My social media links are as follows:

https://www.facebook.com/Anita.tendulkar.9

https://www.facebook.com/stargalaxy1111

https://www.linkedin.com/in/dr-Anita-Tendulkar-59b92937

JOIN OUR NEXT PROJECT OF AUTHOR COLLABORATION

Standing against the Giant, alone, is frightening.

When you are small and beginning, the Giants will try to strangle you, ensure that you drown. The moment you manage to get a breath, by putting your head out of the water, they will put their feet on your head to ascertain you don't emerge.

They won't celebrate your success; rather think that you don't deserve it in the first place. It's a big, wide, wild world out there and you may feel you are alone facing the entire world.

Writing your book and publishing it is almost the same feeling!

For many of us who are labelled introverts, find ourselves struggling. We wish to be writers and authors but we hide behind a pen-name and express ourselves. We duck behind the cozy computer and simply write, pour our hearts out. Ah...if only, if only.

Leading and collaborating a group of authors and promising them that their book will be the number one Bestseller is not a small resolution.

They have high hopes in you and trust you with the process.

They open up their vulnerabilities and allow the world to see those because they believe in you.

One needs to be courageous to be an author, to let the world see your vulnerability you need to be gallant.

But I know for a fact that the big wide world looks less frightening when we do this together. Every fear seems small when we join hands. Together, we celebrate each other's success, we wipe away each other's tears, we pat each other's back, and we know we have each other.

Would you join me for the Next Book Collaboration Project?

You don't need to be a writer.

You don't need to come up with a big buck.

You don't need to have a lot of resources.

You don't even have to worry about the process.

All we need is for you to pick up your courage and join us to tell your story.

Send us an email at Contact@twisbpublishing.com

MY GRATITUDE

A book doesn't come together on its own!

I couldn't have made it without my friends and the great team behind which made this Book Collaboration Project, a success.

Thank you to all the 17 Authors that decided to give me this opportunity to publish their stories through this book project.

Their courage of taking the first step to tell their stories in this book, stories they never told anyone before is commendable. Their stories will inspire others to come forward to tell their stories too.

Angela Mah. Dr. Anita. Dr. Ankit Agur
Archana Chawla. Chrissy G. Tasker. Dee Khanduja
Ho Ee Kid. Ian Maxwell. Jenny Wang. May Quan Ho
Meenu Agrawal. Monika Khanna. Nishith Bhatnagar
Karen Saunders. Sargun Bedi. Tammie Horton. Vinson
Chua .Vera Lim

Thank you to all and I love you so much!!

 Thank you, **Angela and Keziah**, in Dec 2019 we bet and promised each other to publish our book in the year 2020. Look how far we come!
Thank you, **Sargun Bedi**, for gifting us the beautiful Marketing Video. Thank you for your constant support and all the excellent idea you shared with me from creating to marketing the book. I truly value your friendship, Mate!

Thank you, **Dee Khanduja**, for the fabulous write up of the book introduction on the cover page. Thank you for helping us to get on the Expat Magazine, and it has been such a fantastic opportunity for our book to have media exposure to reach more reader.

"There is no value in the things we are doing if they are not done in love. Generosity without love is empty. The greatest deed done without love is nothing. The only right motive for doing what we do is true love."

Thank you, **Rev. Dr. Christopher Chern**, for the Gracing the book with the beautiful Foreword. May God continues to bless you, your family and your ministries.

Thanks to Everyone at ***The World is so big Publishing***: Cynthia, Cally, John, Haroon, Snitz, Dee, Rebecca, Rahul and Deepika. The book came together beautifully because of the excellent team effort. I am grateful for your help.

Thank you to my Dog Reggie who accompanies me day and night while I write.

Love you all xxx

Chrissy G. Tasker

Founder of The World is so big Publishing

We hope your life blossoms just like our **Garden Of Love** with love, hope, joy, determination, encouragement, confidence, and inspiration!

Thank you for being a part of our journey.

Available on Amazon

viewbook.at/GardenOfHope

For more information on Book Collaboration Project

Please visit

www.twisbpublishing.com